ROAD BIKE
Asheville
North Carolina

FAVORITE RIDES OF THE
BLUE RIDGE BICYCLE CLUB

milestone press

almond, nc

© Copyright 1997 by Milestone Press, Inc.
3rd printing July 2006

All Rights Reserved.

Book design by Ron Roman
Maps by Jim Parham

Cover photo courtesy of Cane Creek Components/Bob Allen
Photography

Milestone Press, Inc., P.O. Box 158, Almond, NC 28702
www.milestonepress.com

Library of Congress Cataloging-In-Publication Data

Road bike Asheville, North Carolina : favorite rides of the Blue
  Ridge Bicycle Club.
          p.   cm.
        ISBN 1-889596-00-0
        1. Bicycle touring—North Carolina—Asheville—
Guidebooks. 2. Asheville (N.C.)—Guidebooks. I. Blue Ridge
Bike Club (Asheville, N.C.)
GV1045.5.N752A757 1997
796.6′4′0975688–dc21   97-7823
                                                          CIP

This book is representative of the entire Blue Ridge Bicycle Club. However, without the dedicated work of a team of key individuals, it would likely still be on the drawing board.

Project coordinators were Geoffrey Bullock (1996 club president) and Paul Christopher. The team was held together and directed early on by Geoffrey, and later by Paul. They made sure information deadlines were met and took care of getting materials to the publisher.

The team felt it was important that all the mileages be checked with the same cyclocomputer on the same bike by the same person to help maintain consistency. Ralph Draves took on this job, along with compiling the cue sheets and organizing the information for the elevation profiles.

Mike Byer, Nancy Byer, Wes Garbee, Claudia Nix, David Plunkett, Kevin Stock, Julie White and other members worked together to come up with the route descriptions, difficulty ratings, ride characteristics and cautions, and points of interest.

Finally, we wish to thank Cane Creek Components of Fletcher, N.C. for their contribution of the cover photo. Many top quality bicycle parts are made by Cane Creek and the Asheville area serves as a testing ground for their components. You'll ride past their offices on several of the routes in this book.

Asheville, North Carolina, tucked away in the heart of the Blue Ridge Mountains, is one of America's best kept road biking secrets. It has all the elements that make for great cycling—year-round riding, a wide choice of terrain, and many paved, scenic backroads that see light automotive use.

Asheville is a very cycle-friendly community. A number of bike shops are located right in town, and there are plenty of local riders as well as a general acceptance of cycling among the driving public. It's easy to start a ride downtown and just minutes later find yourself in vastly different rural and scenic surroundings. Access to the scenic Blue Ridge Parkway is easy and virtually immediate. The weather, the views, the local flora and the traffic all change with the seasons, so the same route may be experienced quite differently depending on when it is ridden.

This book contains the favorite rides of the Blue Ridge Bicycle Club, the members of which represent the majority of cyclists in the Asheville area. It also represents years of road riding experience in the region. The routes described here can take anywhere from an hour to the better part of a day to complete, and they should appeal to most any rider on most any kind of bicycle. That's one reason they are club favorites—none are too tortuous, and many take the rider past interesting and historic places. A few routes are offered specifically for the super-advanced level rider looking for a real challenge, but increasing the difficulty rating on just about any of these rides is easy—simply pick up the pace or combine one ride with another to make it harder.

It would be impossible to describe cycling in the Asheville area without devoting some space to the topography. There are flat rides, there are rolling rides and there are mountainous rides, but don't forget—this is the heart of the Blue Ridge. Elevations start at around 1600 feet and range to as high as 6500 feet. Rides local cyclists consider "flat" are sometimes quite hilly and challenging to those used to level, lowland riding.

An equally important aspect of the Asheville area is its climate. You can ride on the road year-round, as there are few very hot or very cold days. Temperatures range widely throughout the year and can vary dramatically with changes in altitude. Sunny, 60°–70° days may occur anytime throughout the winter, although 30°–40° is more common, and a few deep freezes are always expected. Spring and fall are generally moderate and summers can be quite warm with a notable increase in humidity, but the area is significantly less humid than the surrounding lowlands. You can also expect isolated thunderstorms in spring and summer, even on sunny days. They are most common in late afternoon, appear out of nowhere, and usually pass quickly.

Spring is generally regarded as the best time for riding. Expect moderate but warm temperatures and an abundance of blooming wildflowers. The humidity of summer hasn't set in yet, so less moisture in the air makes for much clearer views. As summer rolls around, things really start to green up. Views are not as abundant, but the shade is a welcome relief. Autumn with its cooler days makes for delightful riding. It's also very popular with touring motorists. The "leaf season" lasts several weeks, because the changes in altitude result in color changes starting early and ending much later. An autumn ride may start in green trees and ascend through brilliant colors, topping out at bare-branches in the upper elevations. However, extra caution for riding is required since so many additional autos are on the roads and drivers are sometimes concentrating on the foliage as much as the driving. In winter, you take what you can get.

Generally the road surfaces in the area are excellent. However, gravel resides on the unpaved shoulders and some of it inevitably ends up in the road, often after a heavy rain. Winding, curvy, narrow downhills are especially dangerous in wet conditions. Be aware too, that loose dogs are not an uncommon sight in the rural areas.

This book contains the information you need to get a great start riding in and around Asheville. In selecting your route, first assess your own ability level and then look closely at the distance of the ride coupled with the elevation profile. These two elements can make or break your riding experience. After that, check out the other aspects to best choose your route. If you need the assistance of a bike shop, check the references on page 10—all are good and several are on or near these cycling routes. If you are interested in group rides, you'll find information about joining the Blue Ridge Bicycle Club on the next page. Whatever you do, don't let this book just sit on the shelf. Stuff it in a plastic bag and carry it with you or make a copy of the map and the detailed turn-by-turn descriptions. Then get out and ride.

The Blue Ridge Bicycle Club was formed in 1974 after a community meeting on bikeways planning was held at the YWCA on South French Broad Avenue. Attendance at that first meeting numbered fifty people, including many city officials. It was decided a club was needed to offer organized rides as well as to work on developing a system of bikeways. Claudia Nix, then Director of Health and Physical Education at the YWCA, took over organizing the club, originally called Asheville Bikeways and later changed to Asheville Bike Club. After a survey of Asheville residents failed to increase support by city officials and several applications for state funds were refused, members became frustrated with the process of developing bikeways and focused their attention on recreational rides.

In the late 1980s the club almost died out. Liberty Bicycles, owned by Claudia and Mike Nix, took over the organization and began offering rides from the shop. By 1990 a group of individuals agreed to run the club on its own and renamed themselves the Blue Ridge Bicycle Club.

The club's major fund raiser, the Hilly Hellacious Hundred, was first held in September 1980. A full century and a metric century were offered, with 35 riders in attendance. By 1996 the event had grown to 250 participants and a shorter family ride was available in addition to the full and metric centuries. The club also hosted the League of American Bicyclists' National Rally in 1995. Most of the rides in this book were catalogued for that event.

The Blue Ridge Bicycle Club currently has about 250 members. Many are from Asheville and its surrounding area, but some are from as far away as Florida. Organized rides for both road cyclists and mountain bikers are held weekly. Members also focus on networking for cycling enthusiasts; bicycling advocacy; representing cycling interests to the U.S. Forest Service; trail maintenance; and adopt-a-highway cleanups, in addition to sponsoring rides for various community events. In other words, the club does a lot with and for the community.

Membership is open to anyone. Regular meetings are held the third Wednesday of every month at various restaurants around the Asheville area. If you want to know more about the club or would like to join, do one of three things. Write to Blue Ridge Bicycle Club at P.O. Box 309, Asheville, NC 28812, call Liberty Bicycles at (704)684-1085, or check out the club web page on the internet at http://www.main.nc.us/BRBC/index.html.

he bicycle has legally been considered a vehicle in North Carolina since 1937. Thus bicyclists have full rights and responsibilities on the roadway and are subject to the regulations governing the operation of a motor vehicle, where applicable. North Carolina traffic laws require the rider of a bicycle to:

- Ride on the right, in the same direction as other moving traffic
- Obey all traffic signs and signals, including stop and yield signs and one-way directional signs
- Use signals to communicate intended movements
- Yield to pedestrians and emergency vehicles
- For night riding, equip the bicycle with a front lamp visible from 300 feet and a rear reflector or lamp which is visible from a distance of 200 feet at night

To insure a safe trip:
- Always wear a bicycle helmet
- Carry plenty of liquids
- Avoid biking at night
- When riding with a group, ride single file
- Wear bright clothing to increase visibility
- Be sure your bicycle is the right size for you and keep it in good repair, checking for loose or worn parts regularly

Remember, the bicyclist always loses in a conflict with a motor vehicle. Ride defensively and in a predictable manner to avoid accidents. Be courteous to other drivers. Keep traffic flowing by helping motorists pass you in a safe manner.

Asheville

Liberty Bicycles
1987 Hendersonville Rd
Asheville, NC 28803
704/684-1085 or 800/96B-IKES

Hearn's Cycling & Fitness
34 Broadway
Asheville, NC 28801
704/253-4800

Pro Bikes of Asheville
793 Merrimon Ave
Asheville, NC 28804
704/253-2800

Break Away Bicycles (tandems)
127 Charlotte Hwy
Asheville, NC 28803
704/299-8770

Carolina Fatz
1240 #3 Brevard Rd
Asheville, NC 28806
704/665-7744 or 800/47G-OFAT

Ski Country Sports
960 Merrimon Ave
Asheville, NC 28804
704/254-2771

Black Mountain

Black Mountain Bicycles
108 Black Mountain Ave
Black Mountain, NC 28711
704/669-5969

Hendersonville

Bikeways
607 Greenville Hwy
Hendersonville, NC 28739
704/692-0613

The Bicycle Company
210 South Washington St.
Hendersonville, NC 28739
704/696-1500

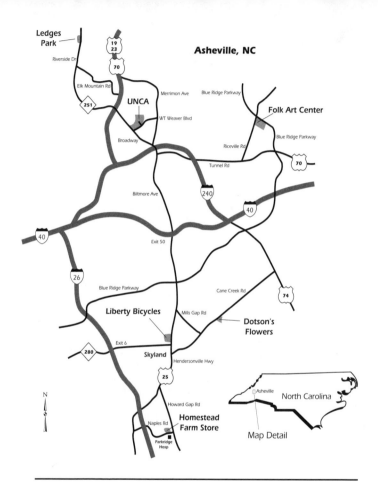

Ledges Park

Riverside Dr

Asheville, NC

Elk Mountain Rd

Merrimon Ave   Blue Ridge Parkway

UNCA

Folk Art Center

W/T Weaver Blvd

Broadway   Riceville Rd   Blue Ridge Parkway

Tunnel Rd

Biltmore Ave

Exit 50

Blue Ridge Parkway   Cane Creek Rd

Liberty Bicycles   Mills Gap Rd

Dotson's Flowers

Exit 6

Skyland   Hendersonville Hwy

Howard Gap Rd

Naples Rd   **Homestead Farm Store**

Parkridge Hosp

Asheville   North Carolina

Map Detail

N

The rides in this book begin at six different starting points: **Ledges Park** on Route 251, The University of North Carolina at Asheville (**UNCA**), the **Folk Art Center** just off the Blue Ridge Parkway, **Liberty Bicycles** in Skyland on Route 25, **Dotson's Flowers** on Cane Creek Road, and **Homestead Farm Store** across from Parkridge Hospital on Naples Road.

Tipton Hill Loop

Rating: Easy   **19 Miles**

This ride is rated easy due to the rolling terrain.

Beginning along the French Broad River, this loop rolls over gentle hills through rural countryside. You can expect plenty of really good views on this ride. From the open farmland valleys, you look up to the surrounding Blue Ridge. Atop several of the climbs, you can see in all directions—something to keep in mind as you spin your way to the top. If it's hot and clear, be sure to bring plenty of sunscreen and lots of liquids. There are few stores on the route.

Estimated Riding Times
- Beginner: 2.25 hours
- Intermediate: 1.75 hours
- Advanced: 1.25 hours

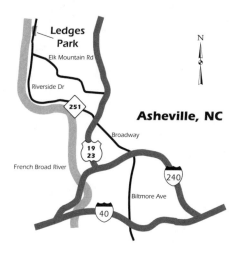

Directions to the Start
- Ride begins at Ledges Park
- From Asheville, take US 19/23 north to Elk Mountain Road exit
- Turn left onto Elk Mountain Road and drive to French Broad River
- Turn right on Riverside Drive
- Go about 3 miles to Ledges Park

Ride Characteristics & Cautions
- Several moderate climbs and descents
- Most of ride is 2-lane country road with rural traffic and minimal shoulders
- Few stores on route—carry provisions
- Open farmland without much shade—bring sunscreen and adequate water in summer

Points of Interest
- Travel through high populations of bluebirds
- 360° views

Mile 4.8
Right on **Tipton Hill**

Fletcher

Knoll Top

Martin

Start
Ledges Park

Tipton Hill

Alexander

Old Hwy 20

Sluder

Jenkins Valley

Ridgeview

Great Views!

Old Hwy 20

F R E N C H

B R O A D

R I V E R

Riverside

251

Bear Creek Rd

N

Mile 11.4
(BP Station) Left on
Old Leicester Hwy

Old Leicester Hwy

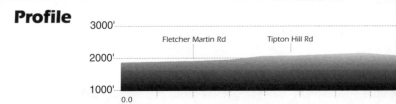

Profile

3000'

Fletcher Martin Rd   Tipton Hill Rd

2000'

1000'

0.0

Map Legend

40	Interstate Highway	●—●	Milepost
74	US Highway	·····	Railroad Track
		▬▬	Route
12	State Highway	──	Other Road
		⌒▲	Direction of Travel

Approximate Scale of Miles

1   0   1

©1997 WMC Publishing. ISBN 1-889596-00-0

For detailed turn-by-turn directions see page 77.

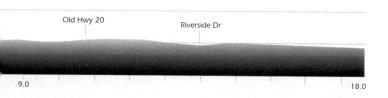

Old Hwy 20

Riverside Dr

9.0

18.0

Cane Creek- Emmas Grove

Rating: Easy

26 Miles

This ride is rated easy because it is relatively flat.

This is one of the flattest rides in the Asheville area. However, you must remember that "flat" is a relative term in the mountains, where nothing is truly level for any sustained distance. Expect gently rolling hills through rural farm country. Along the way is a very pretty valley with many a scenic view.

Estimated Riding Times
- Beginner: 3 hours
- Intermediate: 2 hours
- Advanced: 1.25 hours

Directions to the Start
- Ride begins at Liberty Bicycles. Park in store lot near street.
- From I-26 south of Asheville, take Exit 6 and head east on Long Shoals Road
- Turn left at the third traffic signal onto Hendersonville Highway
- Store is approximately 0.1 miles on left
- From I-40, take Exit 50 onto Hwy 25 south
- Follow for 5.1 miles. Store is on right.

Ride Characteristics & Cautions
- 2-lane winding roads
- Busy traffic early in the morning and late in the afternoon
- 2 brief stretches of Hwy 74A (often with heavy, high-speed traffic)
- Stores and restrooms at beginning and on Hwy 74A

Points of Interest
- Taylor Ranch (longhorn steers)

Cane Creek Emmas Grove

For detailed turn-by-turn
directions see pages 77-78.

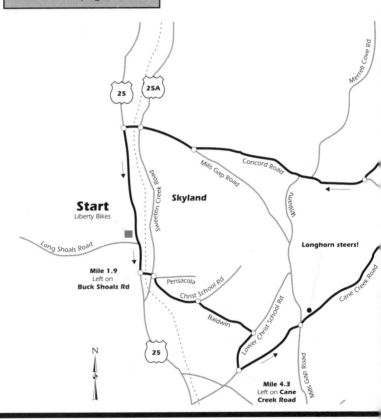

25   25A

Merrell Cove Rd

Concord Road

Mills Gap Road

Sweeten Creek Road

Skyland

Williams

Longhorn steers!

Start
Liberty Bikes

Long Shoals Road

Cane Creek Road

Mile 1.9
Left on
Buck Shoals Rd

Pensacola

Christ School Rd

Baldwin

Lower Christ School Rd

N

25

Mills Gap Road

Mile 4.3
Left on **Cane
Creek Road**

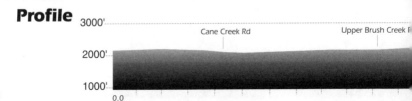

Profile   3000'

Cane Creek Rd   Upper Brush Creek F

2000'

1000'

0.0

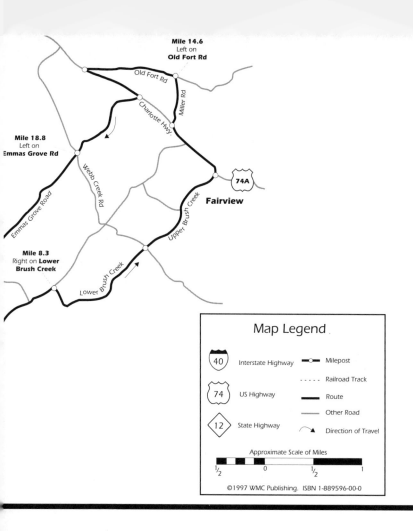

Mile 14.6
Left on
Old Fort Rd

Old Fort Rd

Miller Rd

Charlotte Hwy.

Mile 18.8
Left on
Emmas Grove Rd

Webb Creek Rd

Emmas Grove Road

74A

Fairview

Upper Brush Creek

Mile 8.3
Right on **Lower
Brush Creek**

Lower Brush Creek

Map Legend

40	Interstate Highway	●━●	Milepost
74	US Highway	- - - - -	Railroad Track
12	State Highway	━━━	Route
		────	Other Road
		⌢▲	Direction of Travel

Approximate Scale of Miles

½   0   ½   1

©1997 WMC Publishing. ISBN 1-889596-00-0

Old Fort Rd

Mills Gap Rd

13.0

26.0

Rose Garden Loop

Rating: Easy   8 Miles

This ride is rated easy, but be aware there is one steep climb followed by a fast descent.

This wooded residential route through north Asheville neighborhoods is so quiet it feels like a country lane. You'll want to relax, slow down, and enjoy a leisurely pace as you pass by some of Asheville's loveliest homes and gardens. The middle of the ride is highlighted by a two and a half mile ridge cruise overlooking Asheville and the historic Grove Park Inn. Check your brakes well before this ride—you'll drop off the ridge into a steep, exhilarating descent complete with sharp hairpin turns, ending at a beautiful rose garden.

Estimated Riding Times
- Beginner : 1 hour
- Intermediate : 45 minutes
- Advanced : ride not intended for fast paces

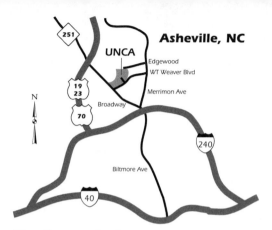

Directions to the Start
- Ride begins at the UNCA Campus upper parking lot
- Take Merrimon Ave to WT Weaver Blvd
- Go 0.5 miles on WT Weaver Blvd to main UNCA entrance
- Upper parking lot is at top of hill on left

Alternate Start: When classes are in session at UNCA start at Covenant Presbyterian Reformed Church on Edgewood Road, 0.3 miles past Belk Theatre just off campus

Ride Characteristics & Cautions
- Most of ride is in residential neighborhoods
- Includes very narrow winding roads with blind curves
- Sustained steep climb up to ridgeline at beginning
- Steep descent with hairpin curves. **Brakes MUST be in good repair.**
- Some steep drop-offs beside road
- Light residential traffic, but be prepared to meet walkers, runners, dogs and other cyclists
- Be aware of sudden intersections on descent—**obey stop signs**
- Road is shrouded with foliage in summer—watch for traffic

Points of Interest
- Community Rose Garden at end of downhill
- Passes historic Grove Park Inn and Country Club
- UNCA Campus and Arboretum

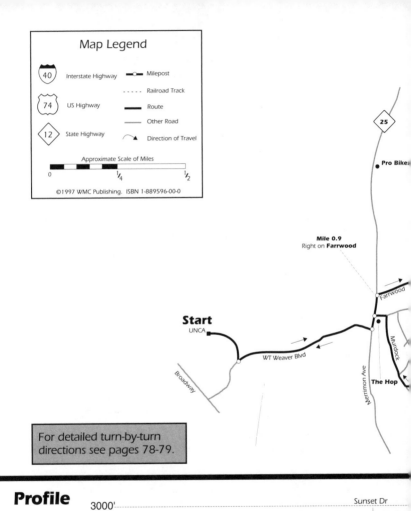

Map Legend

40	Interstate Highway	●━━○	Milepost
74	US Highway	- - - - -	Railroad Track
12	State Highway	━━━━	Route
		──────	Other Road
			Direction of Travel

Approximate Scale of Miles

0   ¼   ½

©1997 WMC Publishing. ISBN 1-889596-00-0

25

● Pro Bike

Mile 0.9
Right on **Farrwood**

Farrwood

Start
UNCA

WT Weaver Blvd

Broadway

Murdock

Merrimon Ave

The Hop

For detailed turn-by-turn
directions see pages 78-79.

Profile

3000'   Sunset Dr

2000'

1000'
       0.0

22

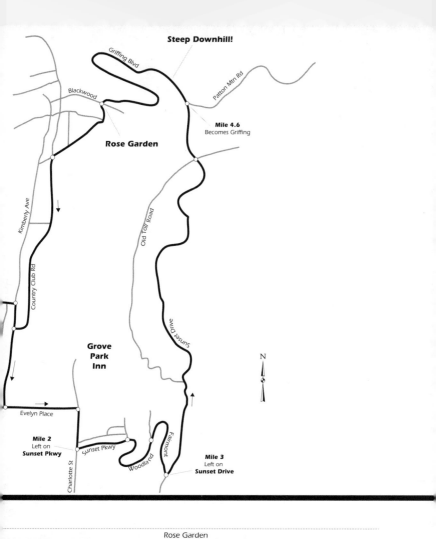

Steep Downhill!

Griffing Blvd

Patton Mtn Rd

Blackwood

Mile 4.6
Becomes Griffing

Rose Garden

Kimberly Ave

Old Toll Road

Country Club Rd

**Grove
Park
Inn**

Sunset Drive

N

Evelyn Place

Mile 2
Left on
Sunset Pkwy

Sunset Pkwy

Woodland

Fairmont

Mile 3
Left on
Sunset Drive

Charlotte St

Rose Garden

4.0

8.1

Breakfast Ride

Rating: Easy/Moderate   17 Miles

This ride is rated easy to moderate because some skill is required on the downhill as well as to manage traffic on the narrow roads.

This ride is an addition to the Rose Garden route. It's fairly easy and passes through the attractive north Asheville neighborhoods—expect to see many large, beautiful homes. For two and a half miles you will ride along a ridge with nice views of Asheville and the historic Grove Park Inn. The climbs encountered are minor and there is one exhilarating, steep descent with sharp, hairpin curves. At the bottom, you'll pass by a block-long rose garden in the median.

Special note: The original breakfast location on this route has closed, but some club members want to keep the ride name just the same. Of course, you can still eat breakfast before or after the ride.

Estimated Riding Times
- Beginner: 2.5 - 3 hours
- Intermediate: 2 hours
- Advanced: 1 - 1.25 hours

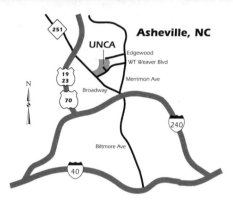

Directions to the Start

- Ride begins at the UNCA Campus upper parking lot
- Take Merrimon Ave to WT Weaver Blvd
- Go 0.5 miles on WT Weaver Blvd to main UNCA entrance
- Upper parking lot is at top of hill on left

Alternate Start: When classes are in session at UNCA start at Covenant Presbyterian Reformed Church on Edgewood Road, 0.3 miles past Belk Theatre just off campus

Ride Characteristics & Cautions

- Most of ride is in residential neighborhoods. Last 3 miles may have busy commercial traffic.
- Includes some very narrow winding roads with blind curves
- Sustained steep climb up to ridgeline at beginning
- Steep descent (start mile 4.6) with hairpin curves. Be aware of sudden intersections on descent in this section.
- Be prepared for frequent encounters with pedestrian traffic, runners, dogs and other cyclists
- Some of the road is shrouded with foliage in summer. Watch for traffic.
- The traffic on Beaverdam Road is deceptively heavy and fast

Points of Interest

- Grove Park Inn
- Rose Garden
- Beaver Dam Lake (half-mile side trip)
- Botanical Gardens at UNCA

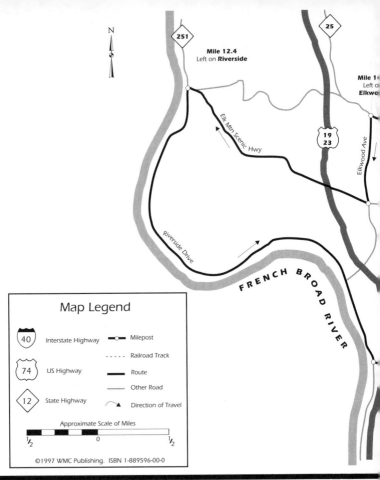

N

251

Mile 12.4
Left on **Riverside**

Mile 1[...]
Left o[...]
Elkwo[...]

25

19
23

Elk Mtn Scenic Hwy

Elkwood Ave

Riverside Drive

FRENCH BROAD RIVER

Map Legend

40 Interstate Highway	⊶ Milepost
	- - - - Railroad Track
74 US Highway	━━ Route
	Other Road
12 State Highway	◞▲ Direction of Travel

Approximate Scale of Miles

½   0   ½

©1997 WMC Publishing. ISBN 1-889596-00-0

Profile

3000' Sunset Dr

Rose Garden

2000'

1000'

0.0

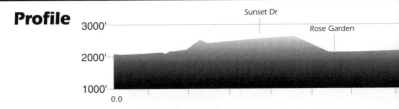

26

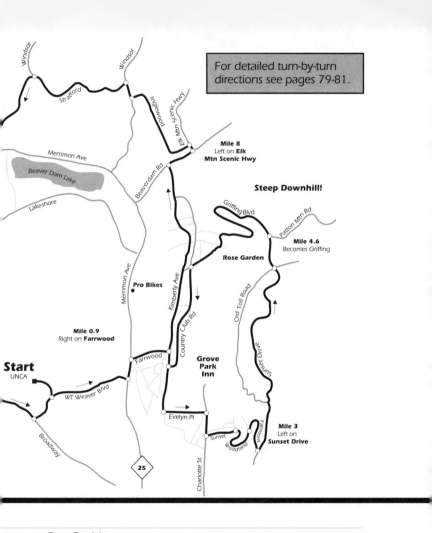

For detailed turn-by-turn directions see pages 79-81.

Windsor

Windsor

Stratford

Merrimon Ave

Inglewood

Elk Mtn Scenic Hwy

Mile 8
Left on **Elk Mtn Scenic Hwy**

Steep Downhill!

Beaver Dam Lake

Beaverdam Rd

Griffing Blvd

Patton Mtn Rd

Lakeshore

Mile 4.6
Becomes Griffing

Merrimon Ave

Pro Bikes

Kimberly Ave

Rose Garden

Old Toll Road

Mile 0.9
Right on **Farrwood**

Farrwood

Country Club Rd

Grove Park Inn

Sunset Drive

Start
UNCA

WT Weaver Blvd

Evelyn Pl

Broadway

Sunset

Woodland

Fairmont

Mile 3
Left on **Sunset Drive**

Charlotte St

25

Beaver Dam Lake

Two Rivers

Rating: Easy/Moderate   **27 Miles**

This ride is rated easy to moderate because of the easy spin along the French Broad River and because of several moderate climbs and descents along the route.

The open terrain on this ride makes for some long range views and a rolling ride with many fun ups and downs. As the name implies, you'll travel beside two rivers. The French Broad is big and wide, and you'll follow it for a good distance. The Ivy River is not so big and you'll ride beside it only a short period. A particularly nice aspect of the route is the gentle downgrade alongside the French Broad. There's also a steep, mile-long climb in the middle of the ride. Be sure to carry plenty of water and provisions; the facilities along the way are limited.

Estimated Riding Times
- Beginner: 3 hours
- Intermediate: 2 hours
- Advanced: 1.5 hours

Directions to the Start

- Ride begins at Ledges Park
- From Asheville, take US 19/23 north to Elk Mountain Road exit
- Turn left onto Elk Mountain Road and drive to French Broad River
- Turn right on Riverside Drive
- Go about 3 miles to Ledges Park

Ride Characteristics & Cautions

- Most of the ride is 2-lane country road with local rural traffic
- Minimal shoulders
- Limited facilities—carry water

Points of Interest

- Beautiful views in Jupiter area
- Riverside parks along French Broad River

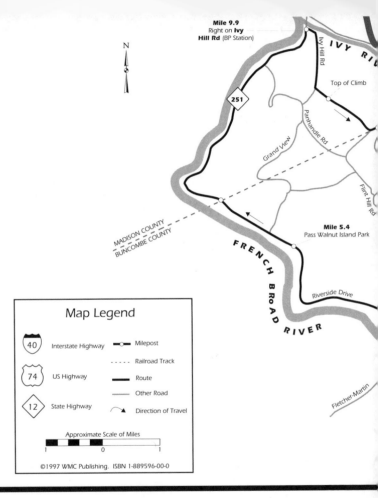

Mile 9.9
Right on **Ivy Hill Rd** (BP Station)

IVY RI...

251

Top of Climb

Ivy Hill Rd

Panhandle Rd

Grand View

Flint Hill Rd

MADISON COUNTY
BUNCOMBE COUNTY

Mile 5.4
Pass Walnut Island Park

FRENCH BROAD RIVER

Riverside Drive

Fletcher-Martin

Map Legend

40   Interstate Highway

74   US Highway

12   State Highway

●—●   Milepost

- - - -   Railroad Track

━━━   Route

━━━   Other Road

⤴▲   Direction of Travel

Approximate Scale of Miles

1   0   1

©1997 WMC Publishing. ISBN 1-889596-00-0

Profile

3000'

2000'

1000'

Ivy Hill Rd

0.0

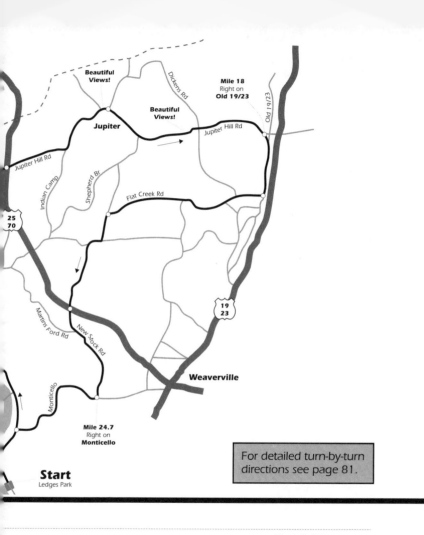

Beautiful Views!

Dickens Rd

Mile 18
Right on
Old 19/23

Old 19/23

Beautiful Views!

Jupiter

Jupiter Hill Rd

Jupiter Hill Rd

Indian Camp

Shepherd Br

Flat Creek Rd

25 70

Martins Ford Rd

New Stock Rd

19 23

Weaverville

Monticello

Mile 24.7
Right on
Monticello

For detailed turn-by-turn directions see page 81.

Start
Ledges Park

piter Rd

Monticello Rd

14.0

27.3

Rolling Vistas

Rating: Easy/Moderate   36 Miles

This ride is rated easy to moderate since it has no major climbs.

An ideal tandem route, this loop remains close to South Asheville for most if its length. About a third of the ride passes through the community business district, while the remainder rolls through rural farmland, and five miles of that is on the Blue Ridge Parkway. You'll see horse farms and have occasional mountain views. Best of all there are no major climbs—a rarity in our mountains! Be prepared to ride on a busy commercial highway for several miles at the beginning and end of the route. The upside to this is that you start from Liberty Bicycles. If you need spare parts, route information or just a pep talk to get you going, the folks in the store are sure to help you out.

Estimated Riding Times
- Beginner: 4 hours
- Intermediate: 3 hours
- Advanced: 2 hours

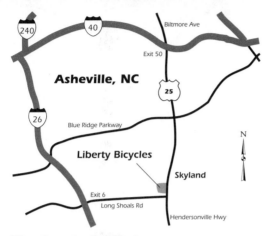

Directions to the Start

- Ride begins at Liberty Bicycles. Park in store lot near street.
- From I-26 south of Asheville, take Exit 6 and head east on Long Shoals Road
- Turn left at the third traffic signal onto Hendersonville Highway
- Store is approximately 0.1 miles on left
- From I-40, take Exit 50 onto Hwy 25 (Hendersonville Hwy) south
- Follow for 5.1 miles. Store is on right.

Ride Characteristics & Cautions

- Several convenience stores and restaurants along route
- 4-lane commercial highway for 2 miles at beginning and end of route
- No paved shoulders
- Often heavy and high-speed traffic on Route 191 (2 sections) and Route 25
- Crossing of 4-lane limited access highway required
- Dangerous intersections (blind curves) getting on and off of Clayton Road

Points of Interest

- Blue Ridge Parkway overlook (info display)
- NC State Arboretum (2-mile side trip)
- Bent Creek Experimental Forest (Mtn. Biking; 3-mile side trip)
- Pottery gallery

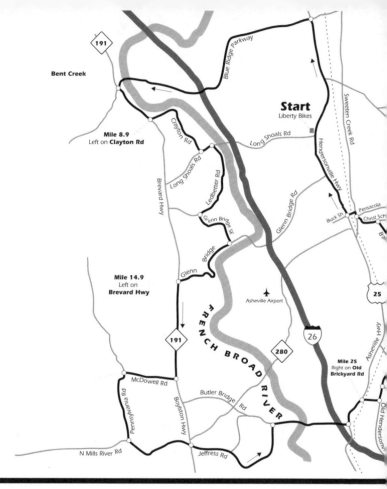

191

Bent Creek

Blue Ridge Parkway

Start
Liberty Bikes

Sweeten Creek Rd

Mile 8.9
Left on **Clayton Rd**

Clayton Rd

Long Shoals Rd

Hendersonville Hwy

Brevard Hwy

Long Shoals Rd

Ledbetter Rd

Glenn Bridge Rd

Buck Sh

Pensacola

Christ Sch

Glenn Bridge SE

Mile 14.9
Left on
Brevard Hwy

Glenn

Bridge

Glenn

Asheville Airport

F R E N C H   B R O A D   R I V E R

25

191

280

26

Mile 25
Right on **Old
Brickyard Rd**

McDowell Rd

Pennsylvania Rd

Boylston Hwy

Butler Bridge Rd

Old Henderson

N Mills River Rd

Jeffress Rd

Asheville Hwy

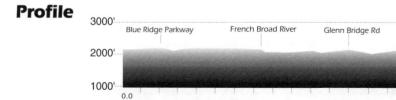

Profile

3000'

Blue Ridge Parkway   French Broad River   Glenn Bridge Rd

2000'

1000'

0.0

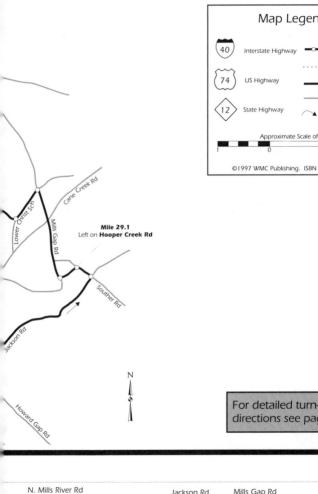

Map Legend

40 Interstate Highway	•—• Milepost
	..... Railroad Track
74 US Highway	▬▬ Route
	—— Other Road
12 State Highway	⌒▲ Direction of Travel

Approximate Scale of Miles

1   0   1   2

©1997 WMC Publishing. ISBN 1-889596-00-0

Cane Creek Rd

Lower Grist Sch

Mills Gap Rd

Mile 29.1
Left on **Hooper Creek Rd**

Souther Rd

Jackson Rd

Howard Gap Rd

N

For detailed turn-by-turn
directions see pages 82-83.

N. Mills River Rd   Jackson Rd   Mills Gap Rd

18.0   36.0

35

Swannanoa Valley & Crafts

Rating: Easy/Moderate   26 Miles

This ride is rated easy to moderate due to the rolling terrain.

Starting at the Folk Art Center on the Blue Ridge Parkway, this ride takes you out to and through the town of Black Mountain—a small village known for its galleries, restaurants and craft shops. Most of the riding, though, is through typical rural Appalachian countryside, complete with the ever-present rolling mountain terrain.

Special note: Timing is important on this ride to avoid the sometimes heavy traffic on Old Highway 70. Look out for school and factory traffic early in the morning and between 3:00 and 4:00 in the afternoon.

Estimated Riding Times
- Beginner: 2.5 - 3 hours
- Intermediate: 2 - 2.5 hours
- Advanced: 1.5 - 2 hours

Asheville, NC

Directions to the Start
- Ride begins at Folk Art Center on Blue Ridge Parkway
- Take the Parkway north from Tunnel Road or use any of the Highway 74 entrances
- Be sure to park in the remote lots, away from gallery

Ride Characteristics & Cautions
- Mostly 2-lane road with drop-offs from pavement to shoulder
- Old Hwy 70 traffic can be heavy at times, especially early AM and between 3 and 4 PM with factory and schools

Points of Interest
- Folk Art Center
- Black Mountain Cherry Street - art galleries, restaurants and antiques
- Warren Wilson College
- Passes near Black Mountain Bicycles

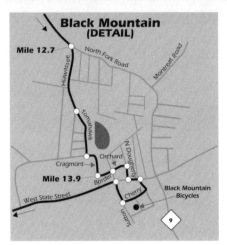

Black Mountain
(DETAIL)

Mile 12.7

North Fork Road

Hiawassee

Montreat Road

Tomahawk

N Dougherty

Orchard

Cragmont

Mile 13.9

Border

West State Street

Cherry

Sutton

Black Mountain
Bicycles

9

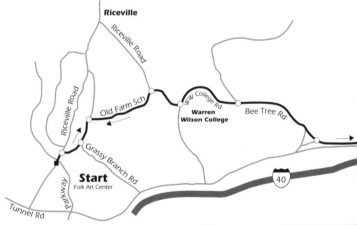

Riceville

Riceville Road

Riceville Road

Old Farm Sch

W/W College Rd

**Warren
Wilson College**

Bee Tree Rd

Grassy Branch Rd

Start
Folk Art Center

Parkway

Tunnel Rd

40

Profile

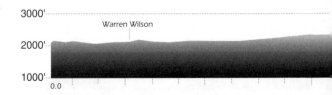

3000'

Warren Wilson

2000'

1000'

0.0

Map Legend

(40) Interstate Highway		•━● Milepost	
		····· Railroad Track	
(74) US Highway		━━━ Route	
		─── Other Road	
(12) State Highway		◤▲ Direction of Travel	

Approximate Scale of Miles

1   0   1   2

©1997 WMC Publishing. ISBN 1-889596-00-0

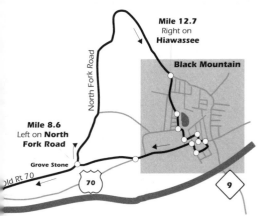

Mile 12.7
Right on
Hiawassee

Black Mountain

North Fork Road

Mile 8.6
Left on **North
Fork Road**

Grove Stone

Old Rt 70

70

9

For detailed turn-by-turn directions see pages 83-84.

Black Mountain   Warren Wilson

13.0   25.7

Ox Creek Plunge

Rating: Moderate   33 Miles

This ride is rated moderate because of the technical skill required to manage the steep descents.

The "plunge" referred to on this ride is one difficult descent with sharp curves found on Ox Creek Road. It's short, but *very steep*. The rest of the ride is characterized by rolling hills leading into moderate but sustained climbs. You'll ride along the scenic Blue Ridge Parkway, through rural farmland and valleys and past beautiful large older homes in residential areas. Much of the ride is shaded, which makes it a good choice on a hot day.

Estimated Riding Times
- Beginner: 4+ hours
- Intermediate: 2.5 - 3.5 hours
- Advanced: 2 - 2.5 hours

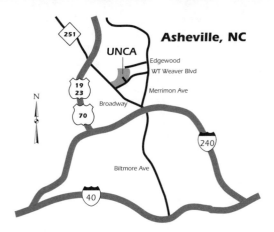

Directions to the Start
- Ride begins at the UNCA Campus upper parking lot
- Take Merrimon Ave to WT Weaver Blvd
- Go 0.5 miles on WT Weaver Blvd to main UNCA entrance
- Upper parking lot is at top of hill on left

Alternate Start: When classes are in session at UNCA start at
Covenant Presbyterian Reformed Church on Edgewood Road, 0.3
miles past Belk Theatre just off campus

Ride Characteristics & Cautions
- Ox Creek Road has one extremely steep descent with sharp
  curves and gravel on the road (and often dogs)—**keep speed
  under control.**
- Mostly 2-lane winding roads
- Heavy traffic likely on last 5 miles of route
- Heavy traffic likely through Weaverville
- Stores and restrooms available at beginning of ride and in
  Weaverville

Points of Interest
- Historic Grove Park Inn Resort
- Blue Ridge Parkway (1 overlook)
- Short side trip available to Vance Birthplace
- Botanical Gardens of UNCA

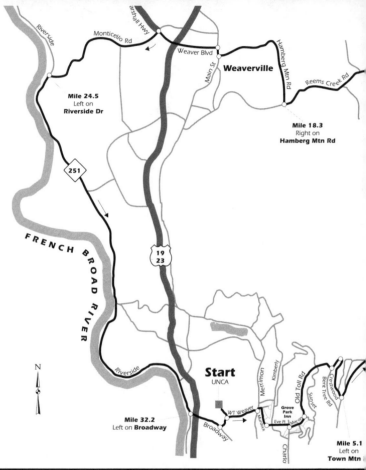

Riverside

arshall Hwy

Monticello Rd

Weaver Blvd

Main St

Weaverville

Hamberg Mtn Rd

Reems Creek Rd

Mile 24.5
Left on
Riverside Dr

Mile 18.3
Right on
Hamberg Mtn Rd

251

FRENCH BROAD RIVER

19
23

N

Riverside

Start
UNCA

Mertimon

Kimberly

Old Toll Rd

Sunset

Crestwood

Brent Tree Rd

Mile 32.2
Left on **Broadway**

WT Weaver

Murdock

Broadway

Charlo

Grove
Park
Inn

Eve Pl

Macon

Mile 5.1
Left on
Town Mtn

Profile

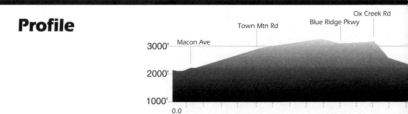

Macon Ave   Town Mtn Rd   Blue Ridge Pkwy   Ox Creek Rd

3000'

2000'

1000'

0.0

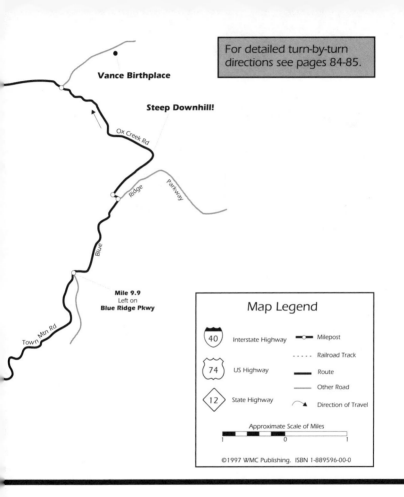

Vance Birthplace

For detailed turn-by-turn directions see pages 84-85.

Steep Downhill!

Ox Creek Rd

Ridge   Parkway

Blue

Mile 9.9
Left on
Blue Ridge Pkwy

Town Mtn Rd

Map Legend

(40)	Interstate Highway	●━●	Milepost
(74)	US Highway	- - - -	Railroad Track
(12)	State Highway	━━━	Route
		━━━	Other Road
		⌒▲	Direction of Travel

Approximate Scale of Miles

1   0   1

©1997 WMC Publishing. ISBN 1-889596-00-0

eemes Creek Rd   Monticello Rd

Main St

Ledges Park

16.0   33.2

43

Jenkins Valley- Ox Creek

Rating: Moderate   **43 Miles**

This ride is rated moderate because of its length and one very
steep climb.

Beautiful countryside characterizes this ride as you pass
through valley farmland set beneath the Blue Ridge
Mountains—it's very pretty. Generally you can expect
rolling hills, but there is also one very steep climb. You'll
travel through the small town of Weaverville's business district and
ride through a brief section of one of Asheville's residential areas on
the return.

Estimated Riding Times
- Beginner: not recommended
- Intermediate: 4 - 4.5 hours
- Advanced: 3 - 3.5 hours

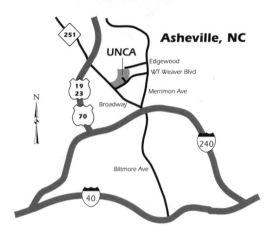

Directions to the Start
- Ride begins at the UNCA Campus upper parking lot
- Take Merrimon Ave to WT Weaver Blvd
- Go 0.5 miles on WT Weaver Blvd to main UNCA entrance
- Upper parking lot is at top of hill on left

Alternate Start: When classes are in session at UNCA start at Covenant Presbyterian Reformed Church on Edgewood Road, 0.3 miles past Belk Theatre just off campus

Ride Characteristics & Cautions
- 2-lane commercial traffic first 3 miles
- Most of ride is 2-lane winding rural highway
- Occasional dense traffic through Weaverville (4-lane traffic as you enter town)
- No stores or restrooms after Weaverville
- Some steep downhill in residential area from Town Mountain Road into Asheville (miles 30 - 37)

Points of Interest
- UNCA botanical Gardens
- Short side trip allows visit to Vance Birthplace
- Brief time on Blue Ridge Parkway
- Historic Grove Park Inn

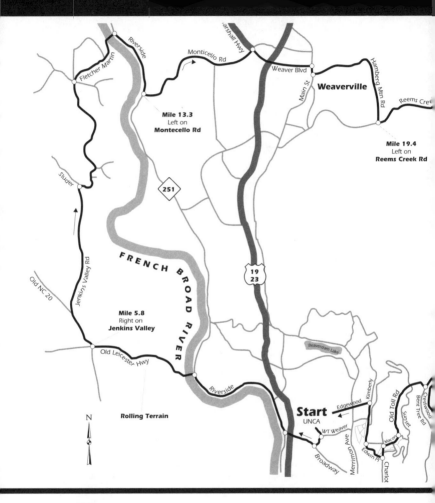

Fletcher Martin

Riverside

Monticello Rd

Marshall Hwy

Weaver Blvd

Weaverville

Hamberg Mtn Rd

Reems Cree

Mile 13.3
Left on
Montecello Rd

Mile 19.4
Left on
Reems Creek Rd

Slutzer

251

Main St

F R E N C H   B R O A D   R I V E R

19
23

Jenkins Valley Rd

Old NC 20

Mile 5.8
Right on
Jenkins Valley

Old Leicester Hwy

Beavertam Lake

Riverside

Kimberly

Old Toll Rd

Brent Tree Rd

Crestwood Rd

Start
UNCA

Edgewood

Sunset

N

Rolling Terrain

WT Weaver

Merrimon Ave

Edwin Pl

Macon

Charlot

Broadway

Profile

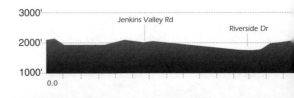

3000'

Jenkins Valley Rd

Riverside Dr

2000'

1000'

0.0

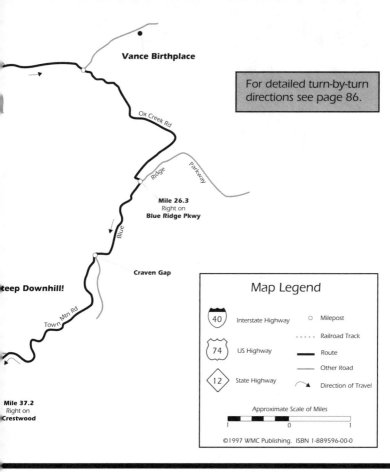

Vance Birthplace

For detailed turn-by-turn directions see page 86.

Ox Creek Rd

Ridge Parkway

Mile 26.3
Right on
Blue Ridge Pkwy

Blue

Craven Gap

Steep Downhill!

Town Mtn Rd

Mile 37.2
Right on
Crestwood

Map Legend

40 Interstate Highway	○ Milepost
74 US Highway	..... Railroad Track
	▬▬ Route
12 State Highway	── Other Road
	➤ Direction of Travel

Approximate Scale of Miles

1   0   1

©1997 WMC Publishing. ISBN 1-889596-00-0

Blue Ridge Pkwy   Town Mtn Rd

Weaverville

21.8   43.2

47

Newfound-Hookers Gap

Rating: Moderate   **32 Miles**

This ride is rated moderate because of one strenuous climb.

The first half of this ride rolls through country valleys and farmland, and the second half takes you through residential sections of the city, past retail stores and light industrial areas. On Newfound Road, expect a scenic, pastoral valley ride. It's a good warmup for the two-mile climb up and over Hookers Gap. The climb is *very* strenuous—it really is, so be prepared. You'll return through the older West Asheville business district.

Estimated Riding Times
- Beginner: 4 hours
- Intermediate: 3 hours
- Advanced: 2 - 2.5 hours

Asheville, NC

Directions to the Start
- Ride begins at the UNCA Campus upper parking lot
- Take Merrimon Ave to WT Weaver Blvd
- Go 0.5 miles on WT Weaver Blvd to main UNCA entrance
- Upper parking lot is at top of hill on left

Alternate Start: When classes are in session at UNCA start at Covenant Presbyterian Reformed Church on Edgewood Road, 0.3 miles past Belk Theatre just off campus

Ride Characteristics & Cautions
- 2-lane commercial traffic for first 2 miles
- Largely 2-lane roads throughout
- Be very cautious crossing Leicester Highway at mile 8.7
- Numerous convenience stores along the route
- Traffic congested on narrow lanes in West Asheville during rush hours
- Easy-to-miss turn onto Hookers Gap Road at mile 13.7
- Be very cautious on the descent after crossing through Hookers Gap at mile 15.6

Points of Interest
- UNCA Botanical Gardens
- Haywood Road through West Asheville is the original east-west corridor through the Asheville mountains

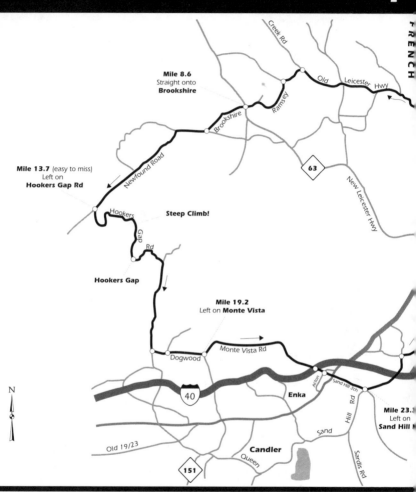

Mile 8.6
Straight onto
Brookshire

Creek Rd

Old Leicester Hwy

Ramsey

Brookshire

63

New Leicester Hwy

Mile 13.7 (easy to miss)
Left on
Hookers Gap Rd

Newfound Road

Hookers

Steep Climb!

Gap Rd

Hookers Gap

Mile 19.2
Left on **Monte Vista**

Monte Vista Rd

Dogwood

40

Enka

Acton

Sand Hill Sch

Mile 23.3
Left on
Sand Hill

Sand Hill Rd

Sardis Rd

Old 19/23

Candler

Queen

151

N

Profile

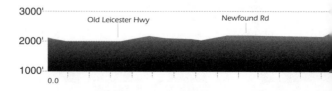

Old Leicester Hwy

Newfound Rd

3000'

2000'

1000'

0.0

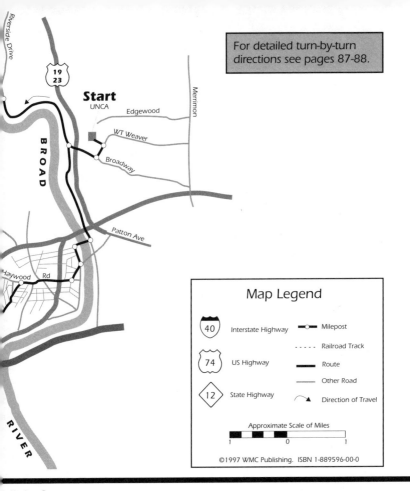

For detailed turn-by-turn directions see pages 87-88.

Riverside Drive

19 23

Start
UNCA

Edgewood

Merrimon

WT Weaver

Broadway

BROAD

Patton Ave

Haywood Rd

RIVER

Map Legend

40   Interstate Highway   ●—○ Milepost

                                     - - - - Railroad Track

74   US Highway   ▬▬▬ Route

                                       —— Other Road

12   State Highway   ◸▲ Direction of Travel

Approximate Scale of Miles

1   0   1

©1997 WMC Publishing. ISBN 1-889596-00-0

Hookers Gap

French Broad River

15.3   31.6

Canton Loop

Rating: Moderate   44 Miles

This ride is rated moderate because of length and one climb worthy of note.

 ou'll ride to the small paper mill town of Canton and back on this route. There is one climb over Newfound Gap, but the majority of time you'll spend cruising over rolling hills and through mountain valleys. There are many nice views. The end of the ride takes you through older West Asheville's historic business district.

Estimated Riding Times
- Beginner: 5 hours
- Intermediate: 3.5 - 4 hours
- Advanced: 2.5 - 3 hours

Directions to the Start
- Ride begins at the UNCA Campus upper parking lot
- Take Merrimon Ave to WT Weaver Blvd
- Go 0.5 miles on WT Weaver Blvd to main UNCA entrance
- Upper parking lot is at top of hill on left

Alternate Start: When classes are in session at UNCA start at Covenant Presbyterian Reformed Church on Edgewood Road, 0.3 miles past Belk Theatre just off campus

Ride Characteristics & Cautions
- Mostly 2-lane winding roads
- Commercial traffic at miles 0-2 and miles 21-25
- Crossing of high speed highway required
- Generally heavier traffic on return half of ride
- Haywood Road (in West Asheville) is a 4-lane, narrow road with many commercial driveways—there can be dangerously dense traffic during AM and PM commutes

Points of Interest
- UNCA botanical Gardens
- Champion Paper Mill

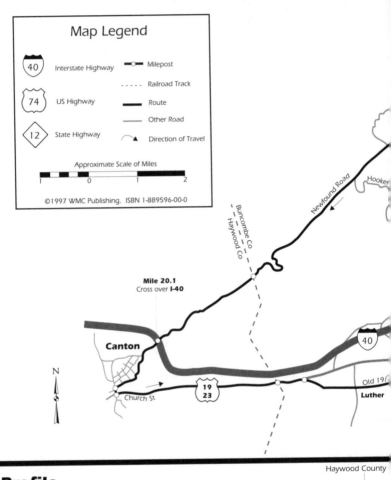

Map Legend

40	Interstate Highway	●━○●	Milepost
74	US Highway	.....	Railroad Track
12	State Highway	━━━	Route
		──	Other Road
		↘▲	Direction of Travel

Approximate Scale of Miles

1   0   1   2

©1997 WMC Publishing. ISBN 1-889596-00-0

Newfound Road

Hooker

Buncombe Co
Haywood Co

Mile 20.1
Cross over **I-40**

Canton

N

40

Old 19/

Luther

Church St

19
23

Profile

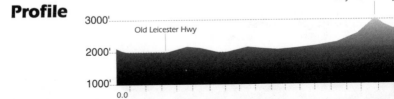

Haywood County

Old Leicester Hwy

3000'

2000'

1000'

0.0

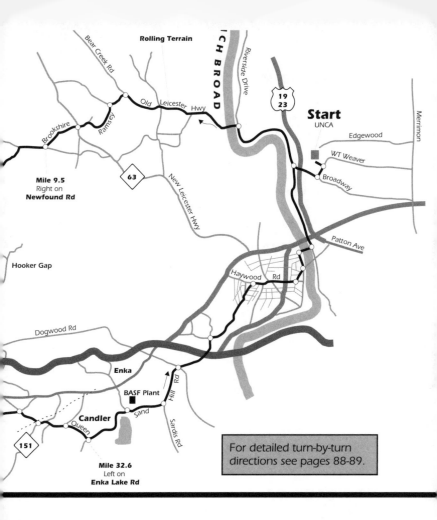

Rolling Terrain

Bear Creek Rd

Old Leicester Hwy

Riverside Drive

19 23

Start
UNCA

Edgewood

Merrimon

WT Weaver

Broadway

Brookshire

Ramsey

Mile 9.5
Right on
Newfound Rd

63

New Leicester Hwy

Patton Ave

Hooker Gap

Haywood Rd

Dogwood Rd

Enka

BASF Plant

Hill Rd

Sand

Candler

Queen

Sardis Rd

151

Mile 32.6
Left on
Enka Lake Rd

For detailed turn-by-turn
directions see pages 88-89.

Buncombe County Line

Sand Hill Rd

Riverside Dr

22.0

44.4

Bear Creek Loop

Rating: Moderate   37 Miles

This ride is rated moderate due to the length of the ride and some technical skill required for descents.

This very scenic and quite hilly ride includes a number of points of interest. Though none of the climbs are real killers, some are long and gradual, so there is plenty of time to enjoy the panoramic mountain vistas. You can expect 15 miles of "mountain flatness" on your return (no road is truly flat in the mountains). You'll then travel through downtown Marshall and past the Rock Cafe, which you may have seen in the film *My Fellow Americans*.

Estimated Riding Times
- Beginner: 3.5 - 4 hours
- Intermediate: 2.5 - 3 hours
- Advanced: 2 - 2.5 hours

Ledges Park

Elk Mountain Rd

Riverside Dr

251

Asheville, NC

Broadway

19 23

French Broad River

240

Biltmore Ave

40

N

Directions to the Start
- Ride begins at Ledges Park
- From Asheville, take US 19/23 north to Elk Mountain Road exit
- Turn left onto Elk Mountain Road and drive to French Broad River
- Turn right on Riverside Drive
- Go about 3 miles to Ledges Park

Ride Characteristics & Cautions
- Entire route is 2-lane rural road
- Riverside Drive is narrow and winding with fast traffic
- Often there are dogs running loose along the way
- Fairly flat return from Marshall to finish
- Steep descent into Marshall with sudden hairpin turn

Points of Interest
- Downtown Marshall Community and Courthouse
- Rock Cafe (used in film *My Fellow Americans*)
- Ledges Riverside Park along French Broad River

Marshall

Courthouse
Rock Cafe

25B
70B

Mile 26.6
Straight

Dangerous
Switchbacks!

Meadowstown Road

Rector Corner

FRENCH BROAD RIVER

Riverside Drive

Madison Count
Buncombe Cour

25
70

Walnut Island Park

Bear Creek

Piney Knob

Alexander Bridge

Fletcher Martin

Tipton Hill

Start
Ledges Park

Mile 1.5
Bear right

Mile 11.8
Cross **Alexander**

Alexander

Jenkins Valley Road

Old NC 20

251

N

Bear Creek

63

Rolling Terrain

Old Leicester Hwy

Profile

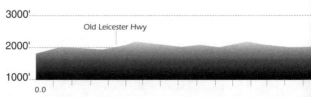

3000'

Old Leicester Hwy

2000'

1000'

0.0

58

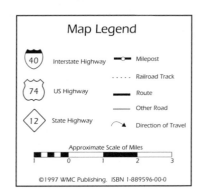

Map Legend

40	Interstate Highway	●━	Milepost
74	US Highway	· · · · ·	Railroad Track
12	State Highway	━━━	Route
		────	Other Road
		◥▲	Direction of Travel

Approximate Scale of Miles

1   0   1   2   3

©1997 WMC Publishing. ISBN 1-889596-00-0

19
23

For detailed turn-by-turn
directions see pages 89-90.

adison County Line

Marshall

Walnut Island Park

18.0   36.7

Carl Sandburg Metric Century

Rating: Moderate   **63 Miles**

This ride is rated moderate due more to length than to terrain.

Be ready for plenty of rolling hills as you ride from small town to small town, past horse farms and alongside the French Broad River. Part way through the route, you'll pass by the famous poet, biographer and historian Carl Sandburg's historic home. When you're done you will have completed a metric century.

Special note: This route has been used for the BRBC's annual Hilly Hellacious Hundred ride, held in late August. The Club currently uses a much hillier course.

Estimated Riding Times
- Beginner: 5.5 hours
- Intermediate: 4 hours
- Advanced: 3.25 hours

Directions to the Start
- Ride begins at Liberty Bicycles. Park in store lot near street.
- From I-26 south of Asheville, take Exit 6 and head east on Long Shoals Road
- Turn left at the third traffic signal onto Hendersonville Highway
- Store is approximately 0.1 miles on left
- From I-40, take Exit 50 onto Hwy 25 (Hendersonville Hwy) south
- Follow for 5.1 miles. Store is on right.

Ride Characteristics & Cautions
- 4-lane commercial highway for approximately first 2 miles
- Most of the ride is 2-lane winding roads, some with drop-offs and few paved shoulders
- Moderate rural and residential traffic
- Crossings of high speed (limited access) highways required
- Numerous stores and restroom facilities evenly spaced throughout the route
- 5 railroad crossings
- Some of route may not be passable after heavy rains. Check at bike shop if in doubt

Points of Interest
- Passes Carl Sandburg Home
- Flat Rock Playhouse

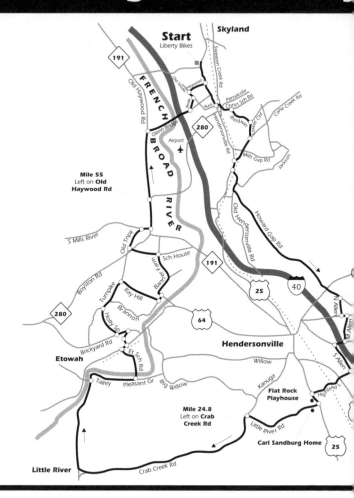

Start
Liberty Bikes

Skyland

191

F R E N C H   B R O A D   R I V E R

Old Haywood Rd

Old School

Haywood

Buck

Glenn Bridge

280

Airport

Sweeten Creek Rd

Pensacola
Christ Sch Rd

Baldwin

Hendersonville Rd

Cane Creek Rd

Jones Cr

Mills Gap Rd

Jackson

Old Hendersonville Rd

Howard Gap Rd

40

N Allen

M Allen

S Allen

Mile 55
Left on **Old
Haywood Rd**

S Mills River

Old Trnpk

Sch House

Banner Farm

191

25

Boyston Rd

Turnpike

Ray Hill

280

Brannon

Holly Sp

Brickyard Rd

Et Sch Rd

64

Hendersonville

Willow

Kanuga

Flat Rock
Playhouse

Highland L

Etowah

Talley

Pleasant Gr

Big Willow

Mile 24.8
Left on **Crab
Creek Rd**

Little River Rd

Carl Sandburg Home

25

Little River

Crab Creek Rd

Profile

3000'

Howard Gap Rd   Flat Rock

2000'

1000'

0.0

Map Legend

(40) Interstate Highway	**—●—** Milepost
	..... Railroad Track
(74) US Highway	**—** Route
	— Other Road
(12) State Highway	⌒▲ Direction of Travel

Approximate Scale of Miles

1   0   1   2   3   4

©1997 WMC Publishing. ISBN 1-889596-00-0

Mile 14.7
t on **North Allen Rd**

na Rd

ward Rd

N

For detailed turn-by-turn directions see pages 90-92.

French Broad   Holly Springs Rd   French Broad

2.0   63.4

Wildflower Bakery

Rating: Moderate   50 Miles

This ride is rated moderate due to its length and the amount of climbing.

This ride gets its name from a really great bakery in the town of Saluda. Since you'll ride all the way down into South Carolina and back up, a stop for refueling at the bakery in Saluda might be a good idea. There are plenty of rolling hills at the beginning and end of the ride, but the main attractions are the *long* descent into South Carolina, the *long* climb through the Greenville watershed and another *long* climb into Saluda and back to Hendersonville. None of the climbs are very steep, just long—really long. If you've got the time there are several short side trips worthy of note—one to the Carl Sandburg Home and the other to the historic Flat Rock Playhouse.

Estimated Riding Times
- Beginner: not recommended
- Intermediate: 4.5 hours
- Advanced: 2.5 hours

Directions to the Start
- Ride begins at Homestead Farm Store (across from Parkridge Hospital
- From I-26 (follow signs to Parkridge Hospital) Exit 13, take US 25 south toward Hendersonville
- After approximately 0.5 miles, turn left onto Naples Road
- Follow 1 mile to Homestead Farms Store on left

Ride Characteristics & Cautions
- 2-lane state highways
- Generally rural and residential traffic
- Some areas of heavy traffic
- Several stores throughout route
- Long fast descent on Hwy 25. Watch for left turn leading to Saluda

Points of Interest
- Carl Sandburg Home (short side trip)
- Flat Rock Playhouse (short side trip)
- Saluda Wildflower Bakery (open Thurs.-Sat.) just off route
- Greenville watershed

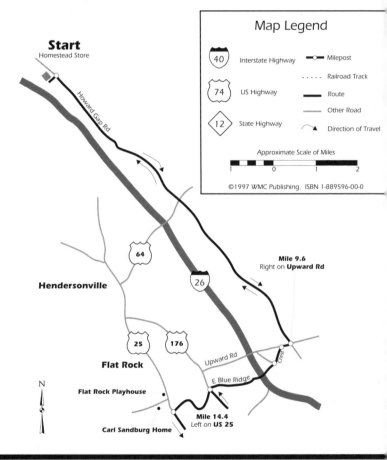

Map Legend

Symbol	Description	Symbol	Description
40	Interstate Highway	⊶ Milepost	
74	US Highway	----- Railroad Track	
12	State Highway	— Route	
		— Other Road	
		➤ Direction of Travel	

Approximate Scale of Miles

©1997 WMC Publishing. ISBN 1-889596-00-0

Start
Homestead Store

Howard Gap Rd

64

26

Hendersonville

Mile 9.6
Right on **Upward Rd**

25 176

Upward Rd

Crest

Flat Rock

E Blue Ridge

Flat Rock Playhouse

N

Mile 14.4
Left on **US 25**

Carl Sandburg Home

Profile

Flat Rock

3000'

2000'

1000'

0.0

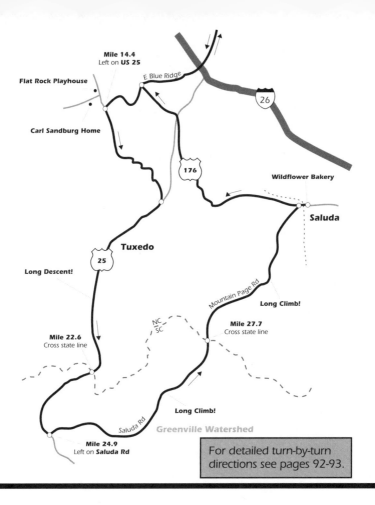

Mile 14.4
Left on **US 25**

Flat Rock Playhouse

E Blue Ridge

26

Carl Sandburg Home

176

Wildflower Bakery

Saluda

Tuxedo

Long Descent!

25

Mountain Page Rd

Long Climb!

NC
SC

Mile 27.7
Cross state line

Mile 22.6
Cross state line

Long Climb!

Saluda Rd

Greenville Watershed

Mile 24.9
Left on **Saluda Rd**

For detailed turn-by-turn directions see pages 92-93.

Saluda Rd

Wildflower Bakery

24.0   50.0

Bat Cave-Edneyville

Rating: Difficult   42 Miles

This ride is rated difficult because of several hard climbs and the technical skill required for the winding descents.

Beautiful mountain roads highlight this wonderful ride through rural apple orchard country. Some of the terrain is rolling, but there are also several long, hard climbs and one six-mile-long, fast winding descent into a river valley. Several side trips are available along the way. However, it is best not to attempt riding into Chimney Rock or on to Lake Lure during the height of the tourist season. If you do, expect alot of traffic. Fall is the best time to get fresh cider at the apple orchards. Members of the club like to use this for a training ride.

Estimated Riding Times
- Beginner: not recommended
- Intermediate: 3.5 - 4 hours
- Advanced: 3 hours

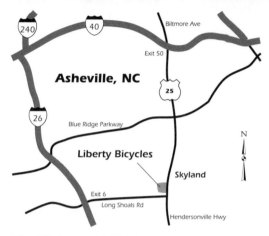

Directions to the Start
- Ride begins at Liberty Bicycles. Park in store lot near street.
- From I-26 south of Asheville, take Exit 6 and head east on Long Shoals Road
- Turn left at the third traffic signal onto Hendersonville Highway
- Store is approximately 0.1 miles on left
- From I-40, take Exit 50 onto Hwy 25 (Hendersonville Hwy) south
- Follow for 5.1 miles. Store is on right.

Ride Characteristics & Cautions
- Winding 2-lane roads, several with severe curves
- Tourist area with heavy traffic likely in Bat Cave area
- Moderate to heavy traffic on Hwys 74 and 64 and Cane Creek Road
- 2 long climbs which can be challenging
- Beware of steep descents, expecially down Hwy 74 from Gerton to Bat Cave
- Watch closely for Mills Gap Road turn, it's easy to miss

Points of Interest
- Bat Cave (restaurants, native arts and crafts, cider mill
- Side trip into Chimney Rock and Lake Lure (filming location of *Dirty Dancing*). Avoid this side trip during peak tourist season; it has **very** heavy auto traffic.
- Apple orchards and cider mills (side trip on Hwy 64)

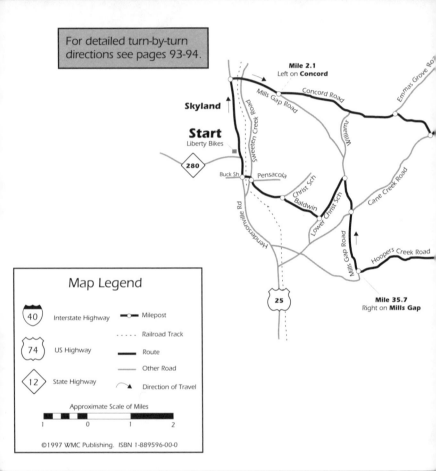

For detailed turn-by-turn directions see pages 93-94.

Mile 2.1
Left on **Concord**

Emmas Grove Rd

Mills Gap Road

Concord Road

Skyland

Sweeten Creek Road

Williams

Start
Liberty Bikes

280

Buck Sh   Pensacola

Christ Sch

Baldwin

Lower Christ Sch

Cane Creek Road

Hendersonville Rd

Mills Gap Road

Hoopers Creek Road

25

Mile 35.7
Right on **Mills Gap**

Map Legend

40 Interstate Highway	●—●	Milepost
	.....	Railroad Track
74 US Highway	——	Route
	——	Other Road
12 State Highway	⌒▲	Direction of Travel

Approximate Scale of Miles

1   0   1   2

©1997 WMC Publishing. ISBN 1-889596-00-0

Profile

Eastern Continental Divide

3000'

2000'

1000'

0.0

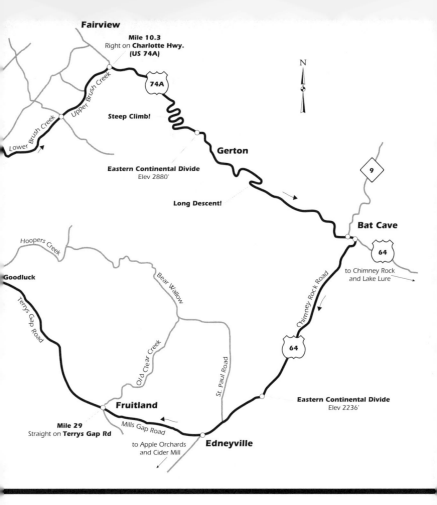

Fairview

Mile 10.3
Right on **Charlotte Hwy.**
(US 74A)

N

74A

Upper Brush Creek

Steep Climb!

Lower Brush Creek

Gerton

Eastern Continental Divide
Elev 2880'

Long Descent!

9

Bat Cave

64

to Chimney Rock
and Lake Lure

Hoopers Creek

Bear Wallow

Goodluck

Terrys Gap Road

Old Clear Creek

Chimney Rock Road

St. Paul Road

64

Fruitland

Mile 29
Straight on **Terrys Gap Rd**

Mills Gap Road

to Apple Orchards
and Cider Mill

Edneyville

Eastern Continental Divide
Elev 2236'

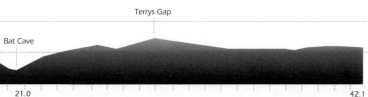

Terrys Gap

Bat Cave

21.0
42.1

Old Fort-Hickory Nut Gorge

Rating: Difficult   64 Miles

This ride is rated difficult due to its length and the number of climbs.

If you want a really gorgeous ride with lots and lots of climbing, one that's very strenuous and lasts all day, this is it! You'll travel through the Hickory Nut Gorge near the town of Bat Cave and under the eaves of Chimney Rock. Lake Lure is not too far away. After the Gorge, it's about twenty miles to Old Fort. A gated road (no motor traffic) takes you back up the Blue Ridge escarpment and into the town of Black Mountain. The climbing and descending is not over yet. You'll climb to Lackey Gap and then down and up several more times before finally completing the loop. If it sounds difficult, it is. It can also be a lot of fun.

Estimated Riding Times
- Beginner: not recommended due to length and climbs
- Intermediate: 8 hours
- Advanced: 5 hours

Directions to the Start
- Ride begins at Dotson's Flowers on Cane Creek Road
- From the intersection of US 25 and Mills Gap Road in S. Asheville, go east about 4 miles on Mills Gap Road to Cane Creek Road
- Turn left and go 3 miles to Dotson's Flowers

Ride Characteristics & Cautions
- Several climbs of varying difficulty
- Very scenic
- Many tourists (not used to mountain driving) on highway
- Traffic sometimes heavy near Bat Cave and Black Mountain
- 3-mile descent with hairpin curves begins at mile 30
- Road up Old Fort Mountain is in very poor condition, but it is closed to traffic (it's scheduled to be improved)
- Very few facilities between towns
- Lots of dogs along route
- If the going's too tough, you can bail out at mile 20.9 and cut 25 miles off the ride length

Points of Interest
- Side trip to Chimney Rock and Lake Lure—if you have the energy
- Several antique shops and unique stores in Black Mountain
- Native crafts in Bat Cave
- Black Mountain Bicycles—one mile off route in Black Mountain

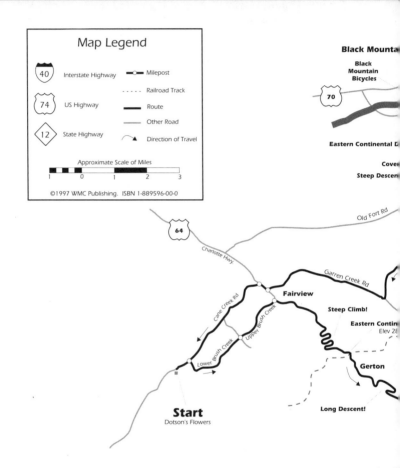

Map Legend

(40)	Interstate Highway	—●—	Milepost
		- - - -	Railroad Track
(74)	US Highway	▬▬	Route
		—	Other Road
(12)	State Highway	⌒	Direction of Travel

Approximate Scale of Miles

1   0   1   2   3

©1997 WMC Publishing. ISBN 1-889596-00-0

Black Mounta

Black
Mountain
Bicycles

(70)

Eastern Continental D

Cove
Steep Descen

Old Fort Rd

(64)

Charlotte Hwy.

Garren Creek Rd

Fairview

Steep Climb!

Eastern Contin
Elev 28

Cane Creek Rd

Upper Brush Creek

Lower Brush Creek

Gerton

Long Descent!

Start
Dotson's Flowers

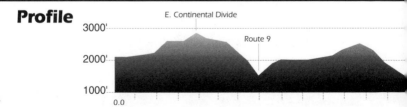

Profile

E. Continental Divide

3000'

Route 9

2000'

1000'

0.0

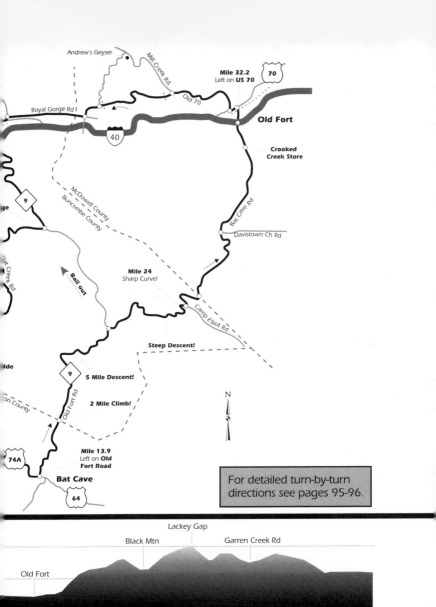

Andrew's Geyser

Mtn Creek Rd

Old 70

Mile 32.2
Left on **US 70**

70

Royal Gorge Rd

40

Old Fort

**Crooked
Creek Store**

McDowell County
Buncombe County

9

Bat Cave Rd

Davistown Ch Rd

Bail out

Mile 24
Sharp Curve!

Camp Elliot Rd

Steep Descent!

9

5 Mile Descent!

N

2 Mile Climb!

Old Fort Rd

on County

Mile 13.9
Left on **Old
Fort Road**

74A

Bat Cave

64

For detailed turn-by-turn
directions see pages 95-96.

Lackey Gap

Black Mtn

Garren Creek Rd

Old Fort

32.0

64.0

75

Tipton Hill

0.0	↰	Exit Ledges Park to the **left** onto Riverside Road (Route 251).
2	↰	Turn **left** on Fletcher Martin Road. Cross bridge just past Alexander Post Office.
3	↱	Bear **right** to remain in Fletcher Martin Road.
4.7	↰ (STOP)	Turn **left** at stop sign on Old Highway 20 (SR 1629).
4.8	↳	Turn **right** on Tipton Hill Road (SR 1627).
6.8	↱ (STOP)	Turn **right** at stop sign on Alexander Road (SR 1620).
6.9	↰	Turn **left** on Ridgeview Road (SR 1621). Expect great views.
8.3	↑ (STOP)	At stop sign, continue **straight**. Road becomes Old Highway 20.
10.8	↱	Bear **right** to remain on Old Highway 20 (SR 1629). Jenkins Valley Road enters from left.
11.4	↰ (STOP)	Turn **left** at stop sign on Old Leicester Highway (SR 1363). Look for BP station.
14	↰ (STOP)	Turn **left** at stop sign on Riverside Drive (Route 251).
14.9	▨	**Caution**: cross railroad tracks.
17.1	↰ (STOP)	Bear **left** to remain on Riverside Drive (Route 251).
18.6	↰	Finish at Ledges Park.

Cane Creek–Emmas Grove

0.0	↱	Turn **right** to exit Liberty Bicycles onto Hendersonville Road.
1.9	↰ 🚦	At traffic light, turn **left** on Buck Shoals Road at Brown's Pottery.
1.9+	▨	**Caution**: railroad crossing.
2.0	↱ (STOP)	At stop sign, turn **right** on Sweeten Creek Road.
2.1	↰	Turn **left** on Pensacola Avenue.
2.1+	↱	Bear **right** on Christ School Road.
2.6	↳	Turn **right** on Baldwin Road (SR 3189).

Cane Creek–Emmas Grove (continued)

3.7	↱(stop)	At stop sign, turn **right** on Lower Christ School Road (SR 3197).
4.3	↰(stop)	At stop sign, turn **left** on Cane Creek Road.
5.1	⤒(stop)	At stop sign, continue **straight** past blinker across Mills Gap Road to remain on Cane Creek Road.
8.3	↳	Turn **right** on Lower Brush Creek Road at Oak Grove Church.
10.3	⤒(stop)	At stop sign, go **straight** onto Upper Brush Creek Road.
12.2	↰(stop)	At stop sign, turn **left** on Charlotte Highway (Route 74).
13.4	↳	Bear **right** onto Miller Road.
14.6	↰(stop)	At stop sign, turn **left** on Old Fort Road. There is no road sign here.
16.4	↰(stop)	Turn **left** at stop sign past the Texaco Station onto Highway 74.
17.4	↳	Turn **right** on Emmas Grove Road.
18.8	↰	Turn **left** to remain on Emmas Grove Road. Webb Creek Road is to the right.
21.2	↰(yield)	At yield sign, bear **right** as road becomes Concord Road.
23.9	↰(stop)	At stop sign, bear **right** on Mills Gap Road.
24.9	⤒(stop)	At traffic light, cross Sweeten Creek Road and continue **straight** on Mills Gap Road.
25.0	▨	**Caution**: railroad crossing.
25.1	↰(light)	At traffic light, turn **left** on Hendersonville Road.
26.1	↳	Finish ride at Liberty Bicycles.

Rose Garden Loop

0.0		Leave UNCA on University Heights.
0.2	↰(stop)	At stop sign, turn **left** on WT Weaver Blvd.
0.7	↰(light)	At traffic light, turn **left** on Merrimon Avenue.
0.9	↳	Turn **right** on Farrwood.
1.1	↱(stop)	At stop sign, turn **right** on Kimberly.
1.5	↰(light)	At traffic light, turn **left** on Evelyn Place.

1.8	At stop sign, turn **right** beside church on Charlotte Street.
2.0	Turn **left** on Sunset Parkway.
2.5	At stop sign, turn **right** on Woodland and begin switchbacks.
2.9	Bear **right** on Fairmont. There is a rock wall on the right.
3.0	At stop sign, turn **left** on Sunset Drive.
3.2	Pass Howland on left.
3.9	At stop sign, cross Old Toll Road and remain on Sunset Drive.
4.6	Road becomes Griffing Blvd. **Caution**: as you pass Patton Mountain Road on the right, you'll begin a steep descent.
5.7	To remain on Griffing, cross Blackwood. This is where you pass the rose garden from which the ride gets its name. It's on the left.
5.9	Turn **left** on Country Club Road.
6.5	At stop sign, turn **left** on Kimberly.
6.9	At traffic light turn **right** on Evelyn Place, then at the stop sign, turn **right again** on Murdock.
7.3	Turn **left** around the Hop Ice Cream shop. At the traffic light, turn **left again** on Merrimon Avenue.
7.4	At the traffic light, turn **right** on WT Weaver Blvd.
7.8	Turn **right** on University Heights.
8.1	Finish at UNCA parking lot.

Breakfast Ride

0.0	Leave UNCA on University Heights.
0.2	Turn **left** at stop sign on WT Weaver Blvd.
0.7	Turn **left** at traffic light on Merrimon Avenue.
0.9	Bear **right** on Farrwood.
1.1	Turn **right** at stop sign on Kimberly.
1.5	Turn **left** at traffic light on Evelyn Place.
1.8	Turn **right** at stop sign on Charlotte Street at

Breakfast Ride (continued)

		church.
2.0	⊢	Turn **left** on Sunset Parkway. This is a divided road.
2.5	⊢ (STOP)	Turn sharply back to the **right** at stop sign on Woodland. Begin switchbacks.
2.9	↗	Bear **right** on Fairmont. A rock wall is on the right.
3.0	⊣ (STOP)	Turn sharply back to **left** on Sunset Drive.
3.2	↖	Pass Howland on left.
3.9	⊥ (STOP)	At stop sign, continue **straight** across Old Toll Road to remain on Sunset Drive.
4.6	⊥	The road becomes Griffing Blvd. Pass Patton Mountain Road on right. **Caution:** steep downhill.
5.7	⊥	To remain on Griffing, continue **straight** across Blackwood. Pass rose and azalea gardens on your left.
5.9	⊢	Turn **left** on Country Club Road.
6.5	⊢ (STOP)	Turn **right** on Kimberly.
7.8	⊢ (STOP)	Turn **right** at stop sign and church on Beaverdam Road.
8.0	⊢	Turn **left** on Elk Mountain Scenic Highway.
8.0+	⊢	Turn **left** on Inglewood.
8.6	↗ (STOP)	Bear **right** at stop sign and country club on Windsor.
8.7	⊢	Turn **left** on Stratford Road, a winding road.
9.5	↖	Bear **left** to remain on Stratford. Windsor is to the right.
10.1	⊢ (STOP)	Turn **right** at stop sign on Merrimon Avenue near Beaver Lake.
10.3	⊢ ▯	Turn **left** at traffic light on Elkwood Avenue.
10.9	⊢ ▯	Turn **right** at traffic light on Elk Mountain Scenic Highway. Cross over Route 19/23. **Caution**: gravel on downhill.
12.4	⊣ (STOP)	Turn **left** at stop sign on Riverside Drive. There are an industrial plant and railroad tracks here.
13.3	↑	Continue **straight** past Leicester bridge to remain on Riverside.
14.9	⊥ ▯	Go **straight** through traffic light to remain on Riverside. This is an industrial area.

15.5	↰	Bear **left** at traffic light on Broadway. Go under Route 19/23.
16.1	↰	Turn **left** at traffic light on WT Weaver Blvd.
16.4	↰	Turn **left** on University Heights
16.6		Finish at UNCA.

Two Rivers

0.0	↰	Exit Ledges Park to the **left** onto Riverside Road (Route 251).
0.9	↑	Monticello Road enters from right, continue **straight**.
1.9	↑	Alexander bridge enters from left, continue **straight**.
5.2	↑	Pass Walnut Island Park on left.
5.9	↑	Cross county line into Madison County.
9.9	↱	Turn **right** on Ivy Hill Road (SR 1589) at the BP Station. Start climb.
10.8	↑	Top of one mile long climb.
12	↑	Cross county line into Buncombe County.
12.9	↑ (STOP)	At stop sign, continue **straight** across onto Jupiter Road (SR 1756). You cross 4-lane Route 25/70.
14.9	↱	Bear **right** to remain on Jupiter Road. Eller Ford Road is to the left.
18	↱ (STOP)	At stop sign, turn **right** on Old Highway 19/23 (SR 2207). This is just before the four-lane.
19	↱	Turn **right** on Flat Creek Road (SR 1764) at Flat Creek Church.
21.5	↰ (STOP)	At stop sign, turn **left** on New Stock Road (SR 1740).
23.2	↑ (STOP)	At stop sign, continue **straight** across Route 25/70 to remain on New Stock Road.
24.7	↱ (STOP)	At stop sign, turn **right** on Monticello Road (SR 1727).
26.4	↰ (STOP)	At stop sign, turn **left** on Riverside Road (Route 251 South).
27.3	↱	Finish at Ledges Park.

Rolling Vistas

0.0	↰	Turn **left** from Liberty Bicycles onto Hendersonville Road.
2.2	↗	Bear **right** on Blue Ridge Parkway access road.
2.4	↰ 🛑	At stop sign, turn **left** on Blue Ridge Parkway heading south.
7.4	↱ ▽	At yield sign, turn **right** on Route 191 at French Broad River.
7.6	↱ 🚦	At traffic light, turn **right** on Route 191 South (Brevard Highway).
8.9	↰	Turn **left** on Clayton Road.
10.2	↰ 🛑	At stop sign, turn **left** on Long Shoals Road.
10.5	↱	Turn **right** on Ledbetter Road before river.
12.2	↰ 🛑	At stop sign, turn **left** on Glenn Bridge Road SE.
13.2	↱ 🛑	At stop sign, turn **right** on Glenn Bridge Road.
14.9	↰ 🛑	At stop sign, turn **left** on Route 191 (Brevard Highway).
16.6	↱	At All Saints Methodist Church, turn **right** on McDowell Road. There's a sign here for Roseway.
17.6	↰ 🛑	At stop sign, turn **left** on Pennsylvania Road.
19.1	↰ 🛑	At stop sign, turn **left** on North Mills River Road.
20.4	↥ 🛑	At stop sign, continue **straight** across Boylston Highway onto Jeffries Road.
22.9	↱ 🛑	At stop sign, turn **right** on Butler Bridge Road.
24.5	↰ 🚦	At traffic light, turn **left** on Asheville Highway (Route 25N). **Caution**: busy highway.
25.0	↱	Turn **right** on Old Brickyard Road.
25.4	↰	Turn **left** on Old Hendersonville Road.
25.8	↰ 🛑	At stop sign, turn **left** on Howard Gap Road.
26.0	↱	Turn **right** on Jackson Road.
28.8	↰	Turn **left** on Souther.
29.1	↰ 🛑	At stop sign, turn **left** on Hopper Creek Road. There is a store here on the left.
29.6	↱ 🛑	At stop sign, turn **right** on Mills Gap Road.
30.8	↥	Continue **straight** across Cane Creek under blinker on Mills Gap Road.
31.4	↰	Turn **left** on Lower Christ School Road.
32.2	↱	Turn **right** on Baldwin.

33.3	←🛑	At stop sign, turn **left** on Christ School Road.
33.8	←🛑	At stop sign, turn **left** on Pensacola Avenue.
33.8+	↱🛑	At stop sign, turn **right** on Sweeten Creek Road.
33.9	←	Turn **left** on Buck Shoals Road.
34	�️	**Caution**: cross railroad tracks.
34+	↳🚦	At traffic light, turn **right** on Hendersonville Road.
36	←	Finish at Liberty Bikes.

Swannanoa Valley & Crafts

0.0	↱	Exit to **right** from rear of Folk Art Center onto Riceville Road.
0.1	↳	Turn **right** on Old Farm School Road.
0.8	←🛑	Turn **left** at stop sign on Grassy Branch Road. There's no sign here.
1.1	↳	Turn **right** on Old Farm School Road.
2.7	↱🛑	At stop sign, turn **right** on Riceville Road. There's no sign here.
3.3	←🛑	At stop sign, turn **left** on Warren Wilson College Road. Continue uphill past college.
4.7	↗	Bear **right** on Bee Tree Road.
6.2	←🛑	At stop sign, turn **left** on Old Route 70. This parallels the new Route 70.
8.6	←🚦	Just past Grove Stone, turn **left** on North Fork Road.
12.7	↳	Just past golf course, turn **right** on Hiawassee.
13.4	↑	Continue **straight** past lake. The road name changes to Tomahawk Avenue.
13.7	←🛑	At stop sign, turn **left** on Cragmont.
13.9	←	To avoid highway, turn **left** on Border Street.
14.1	🛑	Stop sign. Jog across New Bern onto Orchard.
14.2	↱🛑	At stop sign, turn **right** on North Dougherty.
14.3	←🚦	At traffic light, turn **left** on West State Street (Route 70).
14.4	↳	Turn **right** on Cherry Street. There's no sign here. This is the tourist section of town with galleries, stores and restaurants.

Swannanoa Valley & Crafts (continued)

14.6	↱	Turn **right** on Sutton Avenue past the Old Depot Craft Shops and up the hill.
14.7	↰🚦	Turn **left** at the traffic light on West State Street (Route 70).
15.5	↱	Bear **right** on Old Route 70.
19.5	↱	Bear **right** between the two schools on Bee Tree Road. This is the same way you came in.
21	↰	Bear **left** on Warren Wilson College Road.
22.4	↱	Turn **right** on Riceville Road. This is the first road downhill from Warren Wilson Campus.
23	↰	Turn **left** at the top of the hill past the barn on Old Farm School Road.
24.6	↰🛑	At stop sign, turn **left** on Lower Grassy Branch Road. There's no sign here.
24.9	↱	Turn **right** on Old Farm School Road.
25.6	↰🛑	At stop sign, turn **left** on Riceville Road.
25.7	↰	Finish at Folk Art Center.

Ox Creek Plunge

0.0		Leave UNCA on University Heights.
0.2	↰🛑	At stop sign, turn **left** on WT Weaver Blvd.
0.7	↰🚦	At traffic light, turn **left** on Merrimon Avenue.
0.8	↱🚦	At traffic light, turn **right** on Murdock around the Hop Ice Cream shop.
1.1	↰	Take the second **left** onto Evelyn Place.
1.4	↱🛑	At stop sign, turn **right** on Charlotte Street.
1.5	↰	Turn **left** on Macon Avenue. There is a park here on the right.
2.4	↑	Continue **straight** past the Grove Park Inn. Keep right and the road becomes the Old Toll Road.
2.8	↑	Continue on the Old Toll Road as it switches back to the right.
3.7	↰	Turn **left** on Bent Tree Road.
4.5	↱	Turn **right** as the road becomes Crestwood Drive.
5.1	↰🛑	At stop sign, turn **left** on Town Mountain Road. This road is not marked.
8.3	↑	Highest point of ride at 3300 feet.

9.9	←(STOP)	At stop sign, turn **left** on the Blue Ridge Parkway and head north.
11.5	←	Turn **left** on Bull Gap Road.
11.8	→	Turn **right** on paved Ox Creek Road (SR 2109).
11.9	↑	**Caution**: next 3 miles is an extreme downhill. Keep speed under control.
16	↖(STOP)	At stop sign, bear **left** on Reems Creek Road (SR 1003). There is a sign here pointing to Weaverville. If you want to take the side trip to the Vance Birthplace, turn right and ride 1 mile.
18.3	→	Turn **right** on Hamburg Mountain Road (SR 2123). The sign is on the left side of the highway and is easily missed.
20.5	→🚦	At traffic light, turn **right** on Main Street.
20.6	←🚦	At traffic light, turn **left** on Weaver Blvd. **Caution**: this is a busy highway.
21.8	←🚦	At traffic light, turn **left** on Monticello Road (SR 1727). There is a Shell station here on the right.
24.5	←(STOP)	At stop sign, turn **left** on Route 251 (Riverside Drive).
25.4	↑	Pass Ledges Park.
26.8	↗	Bear **right** to remain on Route 251.
29.1	⟍	**Caution**: cross railroad tracks.
29.9	↑	Continue past Leicester bridge.
32.2	↖🚦	At traffic signal, bear **left** on Broadway and go under Route 19/23.
32.7	←🚦	At traffic signal, turn **left** on WT Weaver Blvd.
33	←	Turn **left** on University Heights.
33.2		Finish at UNCA parking lot.

Jenkins Valley–Ox Creek

0.0		Exit UNCA upper parking lot onto University Heights.
0.2	⬏ YIELD	At yield sign, turn **right** on WT Weaver Blvd.
0.5	⬏ 🚦	At traffic light, turn **right** on Broadway.
1	⬏ 🚦	At traffic light, bear **right** on Riverside Drive (Route 251).
3.3	⬏	Turn **left** on Old Leicester Highway (SR 1363) across the bridge.
4.4	↑	Begin rolling terrain.
5.8	⬐	Turn **right** at the BP Station on Jenkins Valley Road (SR 1641).
6.4	⬈	Bear **right** to remain in Jenkins Valley Road.
11.1	⬏ STOP	At stop sign, turn **right** on Fletcher Martin Road.
12.1	⬏ STOP	Cross bridge and turn **right** on Riverside Drive (Route 251).
13.3	⬏	Turn **left** on Monticello Road (SR 1727).
16.0	⬐ 🚦	At traffic light, turn **right** on Marshall High-way (Route 25/70). **Caution**: traffic may be heavy.
16.6	⬆ 🚦	Continue **straight** on to Weaver Blvd.
17.1	⬐ 🚦	Turn **right** at traffic light on N Main Street.
17.3	⬑ 🚦	Turn **left** at traffic light on Hamburg Moun-tain Road (SR 2123).
19.4	⬑ STOP	At stop sign, turn **left** on Reems Creek Road (SR 1003).
21.8	⬐	Turn **right** on Ox Creek Road (SR 2109).
26.3	⬏ STOP	At stop sign, turn **right** on Blue Ridge Park-way.
32.4	⬐	Turn **right** on Town Mountain Road at Cra-ven Gap. **Caution**: steep downhill.
37.2	⬐	Turn **right** on Crestwood.
38.2	⬏	Turn **left** on Bent Tree Road.
38.9	⬏ STOP	At stop sign, turn **right** on Old Toll Road.
40.3	⬑ STOP	Turn **left** at stop sign on Macon.
41.1	⬑ STOP	At stop sign, turn **left** on Charlotte.
41.3	⬐	Turn **right** on Edwin Place which becomes Kimberly Avenue.
42.2	⬏	Turn **left** on Edgewood Road.
42.5	⬆ 🚦	At traffic light, cross Merrimon Avenue.
43.2	STOP	End ride at UNCA.

Newfound–Hookers Gap

0.0		Exit UNCA upper parking lot onto University Heights.
0.2	↱ YIELD	At yield sign, turn **right** on WT Weaver Blvd.
0.5	↱	Turn **right** on Broadway.
1	↱ 🚦	At traffic light, bear **right** on Riverside Road (Route 251).
3.3	↰	Turn **left** on Old Leicester Highway (SR 1363) across the bridge.
4.4	↑	Begin rolling terrain.
6.8	↰	Bear **left** to remain on Old Leicester Highway (SR 1363). Bear Creek Road exits to the right.
7.1	↰	Turn **left** on Ramsey (SR 1302) just before a small bridge.
8.6	✛ 🛑	At stop sign, continue **straight** across New Leicester Highway onto Brookshire Road. **Caution**: be careful crossing highway.
9.5	↱ 🛑	At stop sign, turn **right** on Newfound Road (SR 1004).
13.1	↰	Turn **left** on Hookers Gap Road (SR 1220). S & S Garage is on the left. Begin a steep 2-mile long climb.
15.3	↑	Hookers Gap, top of climb.
18.3	🛑 ↰	Bear **left** on Dogwood Road (SR 1220). This road is not marked.
18.8	↑ 🛑	At stop sign, continue **straight** to remain on Dogwood Road (SR 1220).
19.2	↰	Turn **left** on Monte Vista Road (SR 1224).
22.1	↑	Cross over I-40.
22.5	✛ 🛑	At 4-way stop sign, cross Acton Circle onto Sand Hill School Road.
23.3	↰ 🛑	At stop sign, turn **left** on Sand Hill Road.
24.9	↱ 🛑	At 4-way stop sign, turn **right** to remain on Sand Hill Road.
26.3	↱ 🚦	At traffic light, turn **right** on Haywood Road past Wachovia Bank.
27.5	↰	Turn **left** to remain on Haywood Road.
28.1	↰	Just before bridge, turn **left** on Craven Street.
28.6	↑	Cross bridge over French Broad River.
28.7	↰ 🚦	At traffic light, turn **left** on Riverside Drive.
29.1	〰	**Caution**: cross railroad tracks.

Newfound–Hookers Gap (continued)

30.6	⊢▯	At traffic light, turn **right** on Broadway. Go under Route 19/23.
31.1	⊣▯	At traffic light, turn **left** on WT Weaver Blvd.
31.4	⊣	Turn **left** on University Heights.
31.6		Finish at UNCA upper parking lot.

Canton Loop

0.0		Exit UNCA upper parking lot onto University Heights.
0.2	⇥▽	At yield sign, turn **right** on WT Weaver Blvd.
0.5	⇥▯	Turn **right** at traffic light on Broadway.
1	⇥▯	At traffic light, bear **right** on Riverside Road (Route 251).
3.3	⊣	Turn **left** on Old Leicester Highway (SR 1363) across the bridge.
4.4	↑	Begin rolling terrain.
6.8	↖	Bear **left** to remain on Old Leicester Highway. Bear Creek is to the right.
7.1	⊣	Turn **left** on Ramsey (SR 1302) just before a small bridge.
8.6	⇉⑤⑦⑥⑦	At stop sign, continue **straight** across New Leicester Highway onto Brookshire (SR 1292).
9.5	⇥⑤⑦⑥⑦	At stop sign, turn **right** on Newfound Road (SR 1004).
16.8	↑	Cross county line into Haywood County.
20.1	↑	Cross I-40.
21.8	⊣▯	At traffic light in downtown Canton, turn **left** on Bridge Street. Champion Paper Mill is up ahead.
22	⇤▯	At traffic light, turn **left** on Church Street (Route 19/23).
26.1	↑	Cross county line into Buncombe County.
26.3	⇟▽	At yield sign, bear **right** onto Old 19/23. The sign is on the left side of the road.
29.6	⇟	Bear **right** at DeGroats Grocery Store onto Candler Elementary School Road.
30.4	▨	**Caution**: cross railroad tracks.
30.4+	⇤⑤⑦⑥⑦	At stop sign, turn **left** on Route 251.

30.5	↗	At store bear **right**, cross 2 small bridges, then take an **immediate left**.
31.4	↦	Turn **right** on Queen Road (SR 3447).
32.6	← (STOP)	At stop sign, turn **left** on Enka Lake Road past the school.
33.9	↱ 🚦	At traffic light, turn **right** on Sand Hill Road past the BASF Plant. There is no road sign here.
35.1	↰ 🚦	At traffic light, bear **left** to remain on Sand Hill Road. Sardis Road is to the right.
35.9	↕	Pass Oak Forest Presbyterian Church and cross intersection to remain on Sand Hill Road.
37.6	↦ (STOP)	Turn **right** at 4-way stop sign to remain on Sand Hill Road.
38.9	↱ 🚦	At traffic light, turn **right** on Haywood Road past Wachovia Bank.
40.1	↤	Turn **left** to remain on Haywood Road.
40.7	↤	Just before bridge, turn **left** on Craven Street.
41.2	↑	Cross bridge over French Broad River.
41.4	↤ 🚦	At traffic light, turn **left** on Riverside Drive.
41.7	▨	**Caution**: cross railroad tracks.
43.2	↦ 🚦	At traffic light, turn **right** on Broadway. Go under Route 19/23.
43.8	↤ 🚦	At traffic light, turn **left** on WT Weaver Blvd.
44.1	↤	Turn **left** on University Heights.
44.4		Finish at UNCA upper parking lot.

Bear Creek

0.0	↱	Exit Ledges Park to the **right** on Riverside Drive (Route 251).
1.5	↗	Bear **right** on Route 251 South.
3.7	▨	**Caution**: cross railroad tracks.
4.6	↦	Turn **right** on Old Leicester Highway and cross the bridge.
5.7	↑	Begin rolling terrain.
7.1	↑	At BP Station continue **straight.** Jenkins Valley Road enters from the right.
8.1	↗	Bear **right** on Bear Creek.

Bear Creek (continued)

11.8	‡(STOP)	Cross Alexander Road (SR 1620) at stop sign.
15.5	↗	Bear **right** to remain on Bear Creek.
17.2	↑	Cross county line into Madison County.
17.5	↦	Turn **right** on Rector Corner (SR 1116). There's no sign, but there is a sign for Antioch Baptist Church.
20.1	↗	Bear **right** to remain on Rector Corner.
20.9	↑	**Caution**: begin descent into Marshall. There are dangerous switchbacks ahead.
23.6	↦(STOP)	Turn **right** at stop sign on Meadows Town Road (SR 1001).
24.1	▨	**Caution**: cross railroad tracks.
24.1+	↦▣	Turn **right** at traffic light on Route 25/70 Business. Pass Madison County Courthouse and the Rock Cafe.
26.6	↑	Continue **straight** at the junction of Route 251.
31.5	↑	Continue **straight** past Walnut Island Park.
34.7	↑	Continue **straight** past Alexander Bridge.
36.7	↦	Finish at Ledges Park.

Carl Sandberg Metric Century

0.0	↦	Exit Liberty Bicycles to the **right** onto Hendersonville Road.
1.9	↤▣	Turn **left** at traffic light on Buck Shoals Road.
2	▨	**Caution**: cross railroad tracks.
2+	↦(STOP)	At stop sign, turn **right** on Sweeten Creek Road.
2.1	↤	Turn **left** on Pensacola then **right** on Christ School Road.
2.6	↦	Turn **right** on Baldwin Road at Crown Cork and Seal.
3.7	↦(STOP)	At stop sign, turn **right** on Lower Christ School Road. There's no road sign here.
4.3	↦(STOP)	At stop sign, turn **right** on Cane Creek Road at Putsch Co. There's no road sign here.
4.6	▨	**Caution**: cross railroad tracks.
4.9	‡▣	At traffic light, continue **straight** across Mills Gap Road to remain on Cane Creek Road.

5.6	←▯	At traffic light, turn **left** on Hendersonville Road (Route 25A).
6.1	↞▯	Turn **left** at traffic light on Howard Gap Road (SR 1734).
6.2	▨	**Caution**: cross railroad tracks.
6.8	⤆	Bear **left** to remain on Howard Gap Road.
13.7	⇟▯	Cross Route 64 at traffic light to remain on Howard Gap Road. **Caution**: heavy traffic.
14.6	⇟⊙	Cross State Road 1734 at stop sign to remain on Howard Gap Road.
14.7	�	Turn **right** on N Allen Road (SR 1746).
15.4	←⊙	Turn **left** on Dana Road (SR 1525).
15.6	⮡	Turn **right** on Mid Allen Road (SR 1893).
16.5	⮫⊙	Turn **right** at stop sign on Tracey Grove Road and then cross I-26.
16.6	↞	Turn **left** on South Allen Road (SR 1756).
18	⮫⊙	Turn **right** on Upward Road (SR 1783).
18.4	⤆▯	Bear **left** at traffic light to remain on Upward Road (SR 1783).
18.6	⇟	Cross US 176. Upward Road becomes Highland Lake Road.
19.2	▨	**Caution**: Cross railroad tracks.
19.9	←⊙	Turn **left** on Greenville Road (Route 25).
20.7	⮡	Turn **right** on Little River Road (SR 1123).
24.8	↞⊙	At stop sign, turn **left** on Crab Creek Road (SR 1127).
32	↑	Continue **straight** on Crab Creek Road (SR 1127) Dupont Road is on the left.
35.4	⮫	Bear **right** on Talley Road (SR 1527). This becomes Pleasant Grove Road.
41.1	↞	Turn **left** on Etowah School Road (SR 1205). Cross bridge.
42.9	▨	**Caution**: cross railroad tracks.
42.9+	⮫⊙	Turn **right** at stop sign on Old Highway 64 (SR1203).
43	←⊙	Turn **left** at stop sign on Brevard Road.
43.1	⮡	Turn **right** on Brickyard Road (SR 1424).
43.5	←	Turn **left** on Brickyard Road (SR 1323).
44	⮡	Turn **right** on Holly Springs Road (SR 1322).
45.1	↑	Continue **straight**. Holly Springs Road becomes Turnpike Road (SR 1328).

Carl Sandberg Metric Century (continued)

46.8	⊢	Turn **right** on Ray Hill Road (SR 1316).
48.9	↰ STOP	Turn **left** at stop sign on Brannon Road.
49	↰ STOP	Turn **left** at stop sign on Banner Farm Road.
50.3	↰	Bear **left** to remain on Banner Farm Road.
51.7	⊣ STOP	Turn **left** at stop sign on School House Road (SR1426).
52.7	⬆ STOP	Continue **straight** across Boyston Road (NC 280) onto Old Turnpike Road (SR 1328).
54	↱ STOP	Turn **right** at stop sign on South Mills River Road (SR 1338).
54.1	↰ STOP	At stop sign, turn **left** on Boyston Road (NC 280). **Caution**: heavy traffic.
55	⊣	Turn **left** on Old Haywood Road (Hwy 191).
57.9	⊢	Turn **right** on Glenn Bridge Road. **Caution**: Watch for sharp left curve on downhill.
61.2	↰	Bear **left** on Beale Road (SR3521).
61.8	↰ STOP	At stop sign, turn **left** on Old Shoals Road.
61.9	⊢ STOP	At stop sign, turn **right** on Heywood Road.
62.3	⊣ 🚦	At traffic light, turn **left** on Hendersonville Road. **Caution**: busy highway.
63.4	⊣	Finish ride at Liberty Bicycles.

Wildflower Bakery

0.0	↰	Turn **left** from Homestead Farms parking lot onto Naples Road.
0.2	↱ 🚦	Turn **right** on Howard Gap Road.
9.6	⊢ STOP	At stop sign, turn **right** on Upward Road. There is a grocery store across the street here.
9.8	⊣	Turn **left** on Crest Road (SR1804).
11.2	⊣	Turn **left** on East Blue Ridge Road. There is a trailer park here on the right.
12.1	⬆ 🚦	At traffic light, continue **straight** across Route 176. East Blue Ridge Road becomes West Blue Ridge Road here.
12.3	⧅	**Caution**: cross railroad tracks.
13.8	⊣ STOP	At stop sign in Flat Rock by the Wrinkled Egg, turn **left** on Route 25 S.

16.9	↰	Bear **left** to remain on Route 25. Follow sign toward Tuxedo.
21.8	↑	Cross South Carolina state line.
24	↤	Turn **left** on Saluda Road. This is the first road on the left after the state line.
26.7	↑	North Carolina state line. The road name changes to Mountain Page Road.
30.6	⟋ ↱ 🛑	At stop sign, turn **right** on Main Street (Route 176) to bakery. **Caution**: Cross railroad tracks.
30.8	↻	Wildflower Bakery—**pig out**. Turn around and return on Route 176.
37.8	↦ 🚦	At traffic light in East Flat Rock, turn **right** on East Blue Ridge Road.
38.7	↱ 🛑	At stop sign, turn **right** on Crest Road. Continue up the hill and cross I-26 on a bridge.
40.2	↱ 🛑	At stop sign, turn **right** on Upward Road.
40.4	↤	Turn **left** at grocery on Howard Gap Road.
49.8	↤	Turn **left** on Naples Road.
50	↤	Finish at Homestead Farms.

Bat Cave–Edneyville

0.0	↤	Exit Liberty Bicycles to the **left** onto Hendersonville Road.
0.9	↦ 🚦	At traffic light, turn **right** on Mills Gap Road.
1.0	⟋	**Caution**: cross railroad tracks.
2.1	↰	Bear **left** on Concord Road (SR 3150). This road is not marked with a sign.
4.8	↦ ▽	At yield sign, bear **right** to remain on Concord Road (SR 3150).
5.9	↤ 🛑	At stop sign, turn **left** on Cane Creek Road.
6.4	↦	Turn **right** on Lower Brush Creek Road (SR 3147) at Oak Grove Baptist Church.
8.4	↥ 🛑	At stop sign, continue **straight**. Lower Brush Creek Road becomes Upper Brush Creek Road (SR 3138).
10.3	↱ 🛑	At stop sign, turn **right** on Charlotte Highway (Route 74). Here you begin a steep climb.

Bat Cave–Edneyville (continued)

14.1	↑	Cross Eastern Continental Divide at elevation 2880 feet. Begin a 6-mile descent.
20.1	↑	At junction of Route 74 and Route 9, continue **straight** on Route 74.
20.3	↦	You can visit the shops in Bat Cave before turning **right** over bridge on Chimney Rock Road (US 64 East). The next 5 miles is a 6% uphill grade.
25.3	↑	Cross Eastern Continental Divide again at elevation 2236 feet.
26.6	↦	Turn **right** on Mills Gap Road (SR 1586) past the Exxon Station.
29	⇕	In Fruitland continue **straight** across intersection onto Terry's Gap Road (SR 1565).
33.4	↰ STOP	At stop sign, turn **left** on Hoopers Creek Road (SR 1569).
35.7	↱ STOP	At stop sign, turn **right** on Mills Gap Road (SR 1586).
37	⇕	Cross Cane Creek Road at blinker and remain on Mills Gap Road (SR 1586).
37.5	↰	Turn **left** on Lower Christ School Road.
38.3	↦	Turn **right** on Baldwin Road.
39.5	↰ STOP	At stop sign, turn **left** on Christ School Road (SR 3188).
39.9	↰ STOP	At stop sign, turn **left** on Pensacola Avenue (SR 3187).
39.9+	↦ STOP	At stop sign, turn **right** on Sweeten Creek Road (US 25A).
40	↰	Turn **left** on Buck Shoals Road.
40.1	⬀	**Caution**: cross railroad tracks.
40.1+	↦ 🚦	At traffic light, turn **right** on Hendersonville Road.
42.1	↰	Finish at Liberty Bicycles.

Old Fort–Hickory Nut Gorge

0.0	↱	Turn **right** from Dotson's Flowers parking lot onto Cane Creek Road.
0.3	↱	At Oak Grove Baptist Church, turn **right** on Lower Brush Creek Road.
2.3	↑ (STOP)	Continue **straight** at stop sign as road becomes Brush Creek Road.
4.1	↱ (STOP)	Turn **right** on Charlotte (Route 74).
8	↑	Cross Eastern Continental Divide.
13.9	↰	Cross bridge and turn **left** on Route 9 (Old Fort Road). Begin 2-mile climb.
16	↑	Cross county line into Buncombe County.
20.9	↱	Old Fort Road. Cross a small bridge. Begin 2-mile climb, followed by a 5-mile descent. **Bail-Out Option**: Stay straight on Route 9 to shortcut the route.
24	↑	**Caution**: At Camp Elliot Road you'll begin a steep descent with a sharp curve in it. Check your speed.
25.9	↑	Cross county line into McDowell County.
27.8	↑	Continue straight as road becomes Bat Cave Road (SR 1103). Davistown Church Road enters from the right.
28.4	↑	Continue straight past the Amoco Crooked Creek store on the left.
32.7	↑	Pass under I-40 and into the town of Old Fort.
33.2		**Caution**: cross railroad tracks.
33.2+	↰ (STOP)	At blinker light, turn **left** on Route 70.
33.5	↱	Turn **right** on Old US 70 (SR 1400) at the sign for Andrew's Geyser-Pisgah National Forest. There is a picnic table here on the left.
35.9	↑	Continue **straight** past Pisgah National Forest Picnic Area sign, across a small bridge and past a dead end sign on the right. **Do not take Mill Creek Road.** **Caution**: The road up Old Fort Mountain is in very poor condition and is closed to motor traffic. The DOT has plans to improve this roadway for cyclists, walkers, etc.

Old Fort–Hickory Nut Gorge (continued)

36.3	↑	Road barricade. There is a grey house on the left. Proceed past barricade to start the gentle climb up Old Fort Mountain.
39.9	↑	Second barricade (watch for broken glass). Continue on same road.
40.9	⊢	Turn **right** on Royal Gorge Road. Do not cross I-40. Continue parallel to I-40 into the town of Black Mountain.
43.3	←┬(STOP)	At stop sign and Hardee's turn **left** and then make a **quick right** to enter town of Black Mountain.
43.7	←🚦	At traffic light, turn **left** on Route 9 South. You'll pass by lots of antique and food shops.
43.9	📷	**Caution**: cross railroad tracks. Leave town on Route 9 south heading toward Bat Cave.
47.9	↑	Cross Eastern Continental Divide at Lackey Gap.
49.5	⊢	Turn **right** on Old Fort Road. Half a mile later look for the covered bridge on the right. You'll make a short steep climb and then a descent. **Caution**: there is a hairpin curve on the descent. You'll turn off this road at the bottom of the mountain.
51.6	←┤	Turn **left** on Flat Creek Road. Look for chainsaw sculptures on the right.
53.8	⊢	Turn **right** on Garren Creek Road to start a gentle 2-mile climb.
60.4	┬→(STOP)	At stop sign, turn **right** on Village Road. There's no road sign here.
60.6	⊢(STOP)	At stop sign, turn **right** on Charlotte (Route 74).
60.7	←┤	At First Citizens Bank, turn **left** on Cane Creek Road.
64.4		Finish at Dotson's Flowers.